HR words you gotta know!

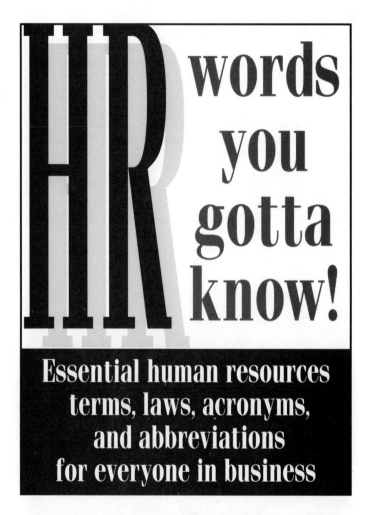

HR words you gotta know!

Essential human resources terms, laws, acronyms, and abbreviations for everyone in business

WILLIAM R. TRACEY

American Management Association

New York • Atlanta • Boston • Chicago • Kansas City • San Fransisco • Washington, D.C.
Brussels • Toronto • Mexico City • Tokyo

Library of Congress Cataloging-in-Publication Data

Tracey, William R.
    HR words you gotta know!: essential human resources terms,
    laws, acronyms, and abbreviations for everyone in business /
    William R. Tracey.
        p.   cm.
    ISBN 0-8144-7856-5

93-74626
CIP

© 1994 AMACOM, a division of
American Management Association, New York.
All rights reserved.
Printed in the United States of America.

This publication may not be reproduced,
stored in a retrieval system,
or transmitted in whole or in part,
in any form or by any means, electronic,
mechanical, photocopying, recording, or otherwise,
without the prior written permission of AMACOM,
a division of American Management Association,
135 West 50th Street, New York, NY 10020.

Printing number

10   9   8   7   6   5   4   3   2   1

For
my
sisters and **brothers**

Mary Josephine (O'Neill) Kirby
James Edward O'Neill
Pauline Rita (O'Neill) Kidik
Margaret Elizabeth (O'Neill) Natale
Eileen Ann (O'Neill) (Tracey) Hendershaw
Francis Xavier O'Neill
John Joseph O'Neill

Preface

The human resources (HR) function is now recognized as one of the most critical areas of American business and industry, as well as one of the most important functions in all types of organizations. In fact, it is a generally accepted maxim that HR has as great a potential impact on competitiveness, productivity, and profitability as any other department, including finance—and much more than many other functions.

The quality of an organization's management is pivotal to its success. Managing is the process of accomplishing the mission and goals of an organization *with* and *through* the work of other people. The manager's task is to establish and maintain an environment that will develop people and facilitate cooperative, effective, and efficient efforts in the attainment of organizational goals.

Anyone who is responsible for supervising the work of others must be directly involved in the processes of recruiting, screening, hiring, training, developing, compensating, motivating, disciplining, and rewarding his or her people. All of those functions are human resources activities. So, not only does HR affect other enterprise operations, it permeates them. HR savvy and managerial competence are inexorably interwoven.

The managers of an organization's financial, production, marketing and sales, and other functional departments are responsible for the most important resource—people. If they fail to recognize this fact and fail to do what is required to maximize the morale, loyalty, job satisfaction, and productivity of employees, corporate trouble begins.

The key to success as a manager or supervisor is to put people first, top down and bottom up. Managers and other key personnel must understand and share employee expectations at all levels. They must do the things that build employee loyalty. They must ensure that clients and customers view their organization as people-centered and caring. All of these things relate to quality management and the achievement of a competitive edge domestically, and, where it applies, internationally.

To maximize the potential of the human resources available to an organization, all key personnel must participate in the development and implementation of the organization's people strategy—its human resources game plan. To do that, they must be able to speak the language of HR. They must be able to communicate with the HR manager and his or her staff and with each other using a common vocabulary. And they must go beyond mere comprehension to achieve an understanding of and commitment to the underlying concepts, principles, and practices of HR symbolized in its terminology.

More specifically, managers and supervisors in all departments of an organization need to understand and use the language of HR if they are to be able to communicate effectively with HR managers and specialists in the following key areas:

- Planning for organization restructuring and dealing with mergers and takeovers
- Linking people goals, objectives, plans, and programs to the company's strategic plan
- Attracting, motivating, and retaining a qualified and competent work force
- Retaining and redeploying people
- Improving the productivity of people and, in turn, the quality of products and services
- Dealing sensitively, compassionately, and successfully with employee performance problems
- Cultivating ethical behavior and teamwork
- Formulating and executing plans for their own training and development

This wordbook of human resources acronyms, abbreviations, and terms and their definitions offers managers the information they need to make sense of the complex, fast-moving world of human resources. It contains more than 1,100 entries, including more than 200 acronyms and abbreviations, over 900 terms, and 83 important employment-related laws. Each entry explains the context and application of an acronym, abbreviation, or term.

The book contains brief definitions of the terms that apply to the HR function in business, industry, government, education, and other nonprofit organizations. At first glance, many of the words included appear to be terms that are common and generally understood. However, some common words have uncommon meanings—their usage is unique to the HR discipline.

The author has often had to make arbitrary decisions on the inclusion of terms and their definitions. Inevitably, some users will disagree with the definition given a particular term. In some cases, they may find more complete information on the term in a standard HR text or reference work.

The book presents entries in alphabetical order. Whenever necessary or helpful, important entries found elsewhere in the book are set in boldface type *within* the definition of a term, and liberal use is made of *See also* suggestions.

This book is the product of several other people. I am in their debt. Special thanks go to Adrienne Hickey, Senior Acquisitions & Planning Editor, and Richard Gatjens, Associate Editor, of AMACOM, and Julie Caldwell, copy editor.

W.R.T.

A

AA	Affirmative action.
AAP	Affirmative action plan.
ABA	Architectural Barriers Act of 1968.
ABP	Account balance pension.
ACUR	Ambulatory care utilization review.
ADA	Americans with Disabilities Act of 1990.
ADEA	Age Discrimination in Employment Act of 1967.
ADLs	Activities of daily living.
ADR	Alternative dispute resolution procedure.
AIA	Anti-Injunction Act of 1932.
ALD	Assistive listening device.
ATS	Applicant tracking system.

ability test In training and development, a test instrument used to measure an individual's physical or mental skills or abilities, such as manual dexterity, reasoning, visual acuity, or problem solving. Examples are Revised Beta Examination, 2nd ed. (Beta-II), Industrial Reading Test, Minnesota Clerical Assessment Battery, Seashore-Bennett Stenographic Proficiency Test, Personnel Tests for Industry (verbal and numerical), and Watson-Glaser Critical Thinking Appraisal. *See also* achievement test; aptitude test.

ability to benefit The likelihood that an individual will complete a program of occupational or remedial training in a successful manner. The ability to benefit may be measured by aptitude, ability, or achievement tests.

absolute ratings Rating systems that require the rater to assign a finite value (on a fixed scale) to the trait or performance being rated without reference to any other person. *See also* behaviorally anchored rating scale.

accessible format Materials prepared for people with disabilities in for-

1

mats other than ordinary print; for example, Braille for blind persons and extra-large print for persons with visual impairments.

account balance pension (ABP) Benefits plan similar to a **defined contribution plan.** Benefits are accumulated in an account to which contributions (based on a percentage of pay) are allocated, and fund earnings are credited to the account under a plan formula. Fully vested participants may receive the account balance in a lump sum on termination of employment; on retirement, participants may take the accumulated balance as a lump sum or in the form of an annuity. *See also* life cycle pension plan.

achievement test A test that measures the extent to which a person has acquired certain information or skills as a result of formal or informal training, experience, or self-study. The most common type of test used by HR managers, it measures the knowledge, skills, and abilities of people in specific subject-matter areas. It is most often used to determine whether a trainee has achieved the learning objectives of a course or training module or to determine the general effects of previous learning experiences, but it is also used in screening and selection to test job knowledge. Commercially available standardized achievement tests, such as the Iowa Tests of Basic Skills and the Stanford Achievement Test, are designed to assess the general effects of previous learning experiences. *See also* ability test; aptitude test; battery.

actives Current workers; preretirement employees.

activities of daily living (ADLs) The basis for determining need for long-term care services. Includes continence (control of bowel and bladder functions), dressing, feeding (taking nourishment), toileting, and transferring (getting in and out of a chair or bed).

actuarially sound In benefits, refers to pension funds that are adequate, considering the amount accumulated in the fund, current levels of contribution, and assumptions made about interest or return on investment, to meet liabilities accrued and accruing.

actuarial reduction A reduction in the amount of earned pension income payable at age 65, applied when a member of a retirement plan retires prior to age 65 and begins to receive pension benefits. It compensates for the longer period of time that such employees will receive benefits than those who retire at age 65 or older.

adaptive media For people with visual disabilities, adaptive media include large-type software and learningware, speech synthesis or talking software, tactile displays, and Braille printers.

adopt-a-country program A means of developing in-house executive expertise to support globalization plans and programs. Participants become expert in a specific country by intensive reading and study of the total culture, language, economy, politics, mores, and traditions and by making frequent visits to the country.

adoption assistance plan Financial assistance provided employees to pay expenses associated with adoption, such as agency, placement, attorney, and other required legal fees, physical exams for prospective parents when required, maternity fees of the natural mother, and temporary foster care charges immediately preceding adoption. May cover adoptions through an agency, private adoptions, or adoptions of children from prior marriages.

adult day care center A center operated by a hospital, nursing home, religious group, or private care organization that provides a variety of health care and social services for people who need assistance for a few hours or all day. Services include grooming and toileting. If licensed by a state and meeting minimum staffing and recordkeeping requirements, its services may be covered by a long-term care insurer. Not covered by Medicare.

adventure training A means of training and developing staff, easing them through corporate change, building teamwork, or strengthening leadership to build trust, delegation, and risk-taking. Adventure training removes challenges people can control and replaces them with genuinely frightening tasks and obstacles that can be completed or overcome only if participants have faith in themselves and their fellow trainees. It is conducted in the wilderness or the woods, rather than in a traditional classroom setting. Participants learn by doing—swinging from ropes, scaling four-story-high trees, white river rafting, running obstacle courses, and engaging in group problem solving (physical problems).

adverse action Disciplinary action in the form of formal sanctions to correct or modify unacceptable employee behavior. Includes written reprimand, written warning, suspension, and termination.

adverse impact The negative effects of employment practices. Although not obviously discriminatory, adverse impacts do in fact affect a protected group differently, significantly, and unfavorably. *See also* protected class.

adverse medical event Treatment by a health practitioner that is designed to help but instead causes illness, injury, or death, whether from surgical or drug administration mistakes, infections, side effects, misdiagnosis, negligence, or incompetence. Also called *iatrogenic injury.*

adverse selection 1. Screening and selection policies and procedures that tend to favor one group over another or affect a protected group differently and unfavorably. **2.** Occurs when an optional insurance plan, such as **COBRA,** is designed in such a way that it will be logically selected by the workers most likely to make the largest claims against the plan.

affective domain 1. Applied to learning, the learner's feelings, attitudes, values, morals, ethics, human relationships, and self-esteem. **2.** Instructional objectives relating to trainees' interests, attitudes, and values. *See also* cognitive domain; psychomotor domain.

affirmative action (AA) In equal employment opportunity, the right of employees, regardless of their sex, religion, race, or physical or mental ability, to be treated equally and without **discrimination** in matters of hiring, pay, and promotion. Also relates to the obligation of employers, as mandated by law, to make positive outreach efforts to assist protected groups to achieve parity in hiring, pay, and promotion to compensate for past discrimination. AA policy has taken two forms: (1) deliberately favoring qualified minorities when hiring or promoting employees and (2) establishing quota systems to regulate the proportion of minority members hired or promoted in accordance with an ideal distribution of employees on the basis of sex, race, creed, or ethnicity. The courts enforce race and sex classifications when necessary to correct past discriminatory practices and patterns. When an employee or labor union is ordered by the court to make concerted efforts to hire minorities who have traditionally been discouraged from seeking employment, the employer is required to to hire or promote additional members of that minority group. *See also* Americans with Disabilities Act of 1990; upward mobility; Vietnam Era Veterans Readjustment and Assistance Act of 1974.

affirmative action plan (AAP) Any company plan designed to correct equal employment opportunity imbalances or the effects of discriminatory practices on protected groups (women and minorities). It usually involves issuing a corporate policy statement; assigning responsibility to a top official; publicizing the plan; determining the status of minority employment; identifying areas of underutilization; establishing goals, specific objectives, and timetables relating to job assignments, functions, and levels, promotions, and compensation; implementing the plan; and monitoring and evaluating progress. *See also* Civil Rights Act of 1964.

age-based defined contribution plan A plan that allows employers to make higher contributions to pension plans on behalf of older key employees, independent of compensation, thereby focusing the dollars on those who will need them soonest. The plan is said to offer the best income-replacement features of traditional defined benefit pension plans and provides the simplicity and flexibility of profit sharing plans. *See also* defined contribution plan.

Age Discrimination in Employment Act of 1967 (ADEA) An act designed to promote the employment of older persons based on their ability rather than age and to prohibit arbitrary age discrimination. The Act makes it unlawful to refuse to hire, discharge, or otherwise discriminate against any individual with respect to compensation, or terms, conditions, or privileges of employment because of age. As amended in 1978, the Act prohibits involuntary retirement because of age in the protected age category 40 to 70 with the exception of (1) **bona fide occupational qualifications** necessary to the business and (2) executives entitled to an employer-provided annual retirement income of $27,000 or more. The Act also proscribes job discrimination in terms of hiring, promotions, and layoffs against workers ages 40 to 70 and applies to employers of 20 or more employees who are engaged in interstate commerce. Effective January 1, 1987, ADEA prohibits mandatory retirement at any age, and the Act continues to prohibit age-based discrimination in all other employment conditions and practices. Formerly the province of the Department of Labor, the Equal Employment Opportunity Commission now has jurisdiction. *See also* Older Workers Benefit Protection Act of 1990; protected characteristics.

agency shop In labor-management relations, an arrangement whereby employees who do not belong to the union must pay union dues because it is assumed that the efforts of the collective bargaining unit benefit all workers, not just members of the union. *See also* Beck case; closed shop; open shop; union shop.

age out Describes children of employees covered by an insurance plan who reach a certain age; for example, age 19 for nonstudents and age 23 for students. Also called *emancipation age*.

age-weighted defined contribution plan *See* age-based defined contribution plan.

alcohol testing Final rules were promulgated by the Transportation Department in December 1992 in response to a congressional mandate passed in 1991 following the Exxon Valdez oil spill in 1989 and several other accidents involving alcohol. The rules became effective in April 1993 and apply to truck drivers, railroad employees, pilots and air traffic controllers, merchant mariners, and others in safety-related jobs. All people starting transportation jobs must be tested for alcohol use before they are hired, and afterward as many as half of them will be subject to random or periodic tests each year. In addition, any worker who is involved in an accident or whose supervisors suspect drinking will be tested.

allowable expense In benefits, any item of expense covered by the benefits plan that is necessary, reasonable, and customary. Such items are typically reimbursable.

alternate long-term care facility A health care facility that provides one or more necessary or medically necessary diagnostic, preventive, therapeutic, maintenance, or personal care services in a setting other than an acute-care unit of a hospital, such as a nursing home or hospice, whether free-standing or part of a life care community. Such facilities provide ongoing care and related services, have a trained and ready-to-respond staff on duty to provide the needed care 24 hours per day, provide three meals per day and accommodate special dietary needs, and are licensed by the appropriate licensing agency.

alternation ranking In job evaluation and performance appraisal, a modified form of relative rating that requires the rater to select alternatively the best employee and then the worst employee from a list of workers until all workers have been appropriately ranked from top to bottom, best to worst.

alternative assessment Means of evaluating educational attainment by other than traditional, multiple-choice standardized achievement tests. Involves direct examination of student or trainee performance on significant tasks that are relevant to life outside of school. Examples include such time-honored means as oral tests, judging actual performance in business education and music, proficiency testing in language, and competency testing for pilots, dentists, auto mechanics, and other professions and trades. Also called *authentic assessment* or *direct assessment*. *See also* performance assessment.

alternative compensation Pay system changes such as skill-based pay, pay for knowledge, profit sharing, gain sharing, key contributor programs, job rates, and lump sum payments. *See also* variable compensation.

alternative dispute resolution (ADR) procedure A procedure designed to settle wrongful discharge claims and avoid costly litigation. The arbitration procedure involves a three-step complaint procedure for any adverse personnel action, other than discharge, and a written complaint step, an automatic appeal to arbitration in termination cases, and a final and binding decision in all cases. Peer review ADR procedures involve use of a peer review board convened for each proceeding in which the employer's challenged personnel decision is reviewed by a board with representation chosen by the employee and management and a facilitator or proctor. *See also* arbitration; expedited arbitration; fact-finding; med-arb; mediation; mini-trial; rent-a-judge; summary jury trial.

alternative work options *See* compressed workweek; flexiplace; flextime; job sharing/job splitting; phased retirement; work sharing.

amateur auditor plan A health care cost reduction program that rewards employees for reviewing their own medical bills and reporting overcharges or other discrepancies.

ambulatory care utilization review (ACUR) A new type of utilization review designed to provide employers with the same type of control over outpatient costs and services that they have over employee in-hospital care. Applicable strategies include **preauthorization**, post-treatment/service auditing, and **physician profiling.**

ambulatory surgical facility Facility that provides surgical services not requiring a hospital stay. It may be independently operated or affiliated with a hospital.

Americans with Disabilities Act of 1990 (ADA) Signed into law by President Bush on July 26, 1990, this Act became effective in 1992. The legislation extends to disabled persons—including persons with hearing and visual impairments, paraplegia and epilepsy, AIDS victims and carriers of the HIV virus, alcoholics, and past users of drugs—the same kinds of protections and guarantees that the **Civil Rights Act of 1964** granted African-Americans and other minorities. That is, employers may not refuse to hire or promote a person who is qualified to do a job simply because that person is disabled. The bill also requires employers to make reasonable accommodations, without incurring a lot of expense or difficulty, to enable a disabled person to do a job. The bill defines a disabled individual as a person with physical or mental impairment that "substantially limits a major life activity," such as walking, talking, or working. It excludes current users of illegal drugs, homosexuals, bisexuals, transsexuals, transvestites, and people with emotional disorders like kleptomania, gambling compulsions, pedophelia, and sexual behavior disorders. It becomes effective after two years for employers with 25 or more workers, and after two additional years for employers with 15 or more workers. The only exceptions will be churches and church-run schools. The legislation classifies alcoholism and drug addiction as medical problems and extends new protections to persons with mental illness and mental retardation and to those with learning disabilities. It requires that employers make the workplace accessible to all employees, forces most public service sector businesses to provide wheelchair access, and requires that buses and a percentage of train and subway cars be modified for handicapped access. Three years after passage, telephone companies will be required to establish relay services between special telephones for people with speech or hearing disabilities and people using ordinary telephones. Regulations will be published and enforced by the Equal Employment Opportunity Commission. *See also* Architectural Barriers Act of 1968; affirmative action; discrimination; equal employment opportunity; protected characteristics; reasonable accommodation.

ancillary medical benefits Dental, vision, hearing, and prescription drug benefits.

andragogy A term attributed to HRD Hall of Famer Malcolm Knowles, androgogy is a way of looking at adult learning. It views adults as needing to be self-directing, as having interests and experiences that can provide a sound basis for learning. It also considers their need to know or to do to fulfill their role in society as linked to their readiness to learn; their orientation to learning as life-, work-, and problem-centered rather than subject-centered; and their motivation to learn as directed by internal factors such as self-esteem rather than by external rewards. *See also* didactic learning/teaching.

anti-cutback rule Provides protection against elimination or reduction by plan amendment of certain benefits provided under a qualified plan. Applies to benefits already accrued under the terms of the plan, early retirement benefits, early retirement-type subsidies, and optional forms of benefits. Does not apply to life insurance, accident or health, Social Security supplements, pre- and posttax employee contributions and direct investments, and plan loans.

Anti-Injunction Act of 1932 (AIA) Establishes and protects the right of employees to participate in union activities by prohibiting **yellow-dog contracts.** It also defines and limits the power of the courts to issue injunctions against certain actions and permits either party to sue if its collective bargaining contract is violated. The law also makes unions immune from antitrust laws (interpreted by the courts to mean when a union acts in its self-interest and not in conjunction with nonlabor groups to achieve its goals). Also known as the Norris-LaGuardia Act. *See also* Weingarten Rule.

any willing-provider law A state law that is a barrier to managed care (14 states currently have such laws). The law permits any provider holding required credentials and willing to conform with the terms and conditions of a network contract to be admitted to that network. Such legislation restricts payers' ability to contract selectively with a limited number of providers to save on premiums. *See also* fair reimbursement law.

applicant files Files initiated upon receipt of applications for positions and files of persons who were nonselected or who withdrew their applications before a selection was made. Although their useful life is relatively short (usually one or two years), they can be a lucrative source of candidates for vacant positions. Sometimes mistakenly called "active" files.

applicant specifications A staffing document that describes: (1) what an applicant for a specific position *should know*—the technical, professional, and managerial knowledge needed to perform the job; (2) what the applicant should *be able to do*—the technical, professional, and managerial skills required to enter the position; (3) what the applicant *should be*—the educational background, kind and amount of training and experience, and the personal qualities essential for success at the entry level; and (4) what the applicant *can expect*—the nature of the job, compensation offered, job functions, duties, authority, and responsibility, position in the hierarchical structure, and potential for advancement. They are used in recruiting, screening, selecting, training, assigning, developing, and promoting personnel. *See also* job description.

applicant tracking system (ATS) A computerized system used to track applicants for positions—from receipt of an application, through the initial interview, to offer and acceptance/rejection—and tabulate evaluations of the organization's recruiting process by the candidates. Some applications provide activity statistics, applicant profiles, custom letters and reports, equal employment opportunity applicant flow, invitation schedules, letter history, past employer retrieval, recruiter statistics, routing status, school and college retrieval, skills retrieval, source statistics, and standard letters.

applied person-day In calculating HR costs and benefits, an employee's cost per applied person-day is that person's full cost per day divided by his or her **applied rate.** The calculation should include training costs incurred in preparing for the assignment. Usually for HR professionals with a 70 to 75 percent applied rate, the applied person-day will equal about four times the direct salary cost per day. *See also* applied rate.

applied rate In calculating HR costs and benefits, a worker's applied rate is the number of hours billed to applied projects or clients divided by the total number of hours paid in a given time period. For HR professionals, it is unquestionably the single most important productivity indicator. For them it should remain in the 70 to 75 percent range. *See also* applied person-day.

apprenticeship programs Developed in the Middle Ages by the trade guilds, the system is used primarily to train laborers, craftsmen, mechanics, and some technicians. A potential craftsperson, such as a cabinetmaker, is "apprenticed" to a recognized artisan for a period of years during which the apprentice learns the skills by observing and performing the work under the tutelage and guidance of the master craftsperson. Although they have declined since the Industrial Revolution, apprenticeship programs remain an important source of skilled workers in the United States. Currently there are about 1,200 apprenticeable occupations. Each state has a director who, together with field representatives, works with state government, business, industry, organizations, and labor to establish and maintain complete training programs. Apprenticeship program standards are established jointly by the organization, and, where appropriate, labor unions, and the United States Department of Labor.

appropriate penalty A legal doctrine pertaining to cases of unlawful discharge. It asks, "Was the degree of discipline administered by the employer reasonably commensurate with the seriousness of the offense and the employee's record of performance with the organization?"

approved charges Medical insurance payments based largely on what the policy (or law in the case of Medicare) defines as "reasonable charges" or the amounts approved by the carrier.

aptitude test Psychological test used in hiring, selecting people for training, and career planning. Similar to tests of general ability but more specialized. Examples of aptitudes are mechanical, spatial perception, mathematics, art, music, and so on, as distinguished from general learning ability. Examples of standardized aptitude tests are Bennett's Test of Mechanical Comprehension, Clerical Abilities Battery, Purdue Mechanical Adaptability Test, SRA Tests of Mechanical Aptitude, Revised Minnesota Paper Form Board Test, and the last four parts of the MacQuarrie Test for Mechanical Ability. *See also* ability test; achievement test.

arbitration A formal form of negotiation used to resolve individual and group disputes including labor-management disagreements. Although it involves a neutral third party, the arbitrator, his or her role is considerably different than that of a mediator. When the parties to a disagreement accept the arbitration process, they also agree to accept the decision of the arbitrator as final and binding. Arbitration is less expensive and time-consuming than mediation or litigation. Enforcement is rarely required because both parties agree before the proceedings to accept the decision, and arbitrators are usually better qualified than the courts to rule on specific labor issues. *See also* alternative dispute resolution procedure; med-arb; mediation; mini-trial; negotiation; rent-a-judge; summary jury trial.

Architectural Barriers Act of 1968 (ABA) An act that mandated the design, construction, or modification of public buildings and facilities owned or leased in whole or in part by the federal government (or financed or aided by federal funds) to provide means of access to handicapped individuals. *See also* Americans with Disabilities Act of 1990; Rehabilitation Act of 1973.

area differential An allowance paid to employees assigned to a foreign country or certain geographic areas in the United States, for hardship factors in the former case and different average pay levels or cost of living in the latter case.

area wage survey A formal or informal survey of the "going rate" for jobs in a particular geographical area used to price benchmark jobs. Surveys may be made by individual companies, professional and technical organizations, and the U.S. government's Bureau of Labor Statistics. The BLS conducts area wage surveys annually. *See also* benchmarks.

Army Employer Network Database An automated help-wanted ad system on-line at 55 Army Career Alumni Program centers worldwide with more than 3,000 employers registered. *Contact:* 800/445-2049 or 703/893-2403.

assessment center A structured method of screening and selecting people for assignment or promotion to executive, managerial, or supervisory positions. Over a period of two or three days, and under the direction of a team of evaluators, participants deal with a variety of realistic management problems and situations. They engage in simulations and business games, **in-basket exercises,** role playing, and decision-making exercises; undergo psychological tests and projective techniques; and engage in group discussion and self-evaluation. Evaluators observe, assess, and record participants' behavior and performance, critique group exercises, interview participants, and combine their appraisals in a formal report. Assessment centers can also be used to diagnose training and development needs. *See also* job sampling.

assignment A process through which a physician or medical supplier agrees to accept an organization's (or Medicare's) payment as payment in full except for specific coinsurance and deductible amounts required of the patient.

assistive listening device (ALD) A device for people with hearing impairments mandated for availability by the **Americans with Disabilities Act of 1990** during all meetings and conventions. Examples of ALDs are infrared and FM systems, both of which can be moved from meeting room to meeting room or permanently installed.

attitude and opinion survey A device designed to elicit information about employee ideas, feelings, attitudes, concerns, expectations, and preferences on a broad range of managerial issues, from problem identification to in-depth analysis of potential problems identified by other means. The survey can uncover the causes of problems, probe feelings about situations or conditions, and elicit ideas for preventive actions.

attrition Usually expressed as attrition *rate*, which is the percentage of trainees dropped from training due to failure to maintain normal progress or achieve established standards.

authorization cards In unionizing, cards used by union organizers to sign up the number of employees needed to petition for a union election (30 percent must sign up).

automated data collection A means of collecting data for work measurement that involves programming computers, whose terminals are used to perform tasks, to record, tabulate, summarize, and report employee performance of those tasks; for example, key strokes per minute, lines of type produced per hour, errors per hour, and so on).

auxiliary aids and services As defined by the **Americans with Disabilities Act of 1990,** "auxiliary aids and services include a wide range of services and devices for ensuring effective communication" (but use of advanced technology is not required), such as qualified interpreters, notetakers, computer-aided transcription services, written materials, telephone handset amplifiers, assistive listening systems, telephones compatible with hearing aids, closed-caption decoders, open and closed captioning, telecommunications devices for deaf persons (TDDs), videotext displays, or other effective methods of making aurally delivered materials available to individuals with hearing impairments. Auxiliary aids and services also include qualified readers, taped texts, audio recordings, Braille materials, large-print materials, or other effective methods of making visually delivered materials available to individuals with visual impairments.

availability forecast Used in HR forecasting. Availability is determined by computer analysis that projects the future capability of the current personnel pool over a specified time frame. The analysis takes into account all anticipated changes in the organization personnel pool due to such factors as projected terminations, hires, and transfers using historical data and statistics to arrive at the projections. *See also* demand forecast.

average final compensation A retirement plan provision that bases retirement benefits on a member's earnings in the years immediately preceding retirement. Typically, the average of the five highest earning years in the last ten years or the highest three-year average is used for the calculation.

B

BARS Behaviorally anchored rating scale.
BBIC Behavior-based incentive compensation.
BFOQ Bona fide occupational qualification.

baby boomers The "thirty-something" generation of post–World War II adults born between 1945 and 1965, who produced the baby boom of the 1970s and 1980s. Also known as *boomers*.

baby busters The twenty-something generation of young adults born between 1961 and 1972—the period when the U.S. birth rate fell to one half the rate of the post–World War II peak, resulting in a labor shortage in the 1990s. Also known as *baby busts*.

balance billing The practice of submitting a bill to the patient for the difference between the original charge for health care services and the amount allowed and paid by **Medicare**. Part B, Medicare, pays 80 percent of the "allowed" amount. The remainder is paid by supplemental (**medigap**) insurance, Medicaid, or the patient. Practitioners can bill the patient for the 20 percent if they have no supplemental insurance. However, it is illegal in some states for practitioners to bill for anything more even if the costs of providing the treatment or service are higher than the amount allowed and received.

base rate The hourly rate or salary paid for a job performed. It does not include payments for overtime, incentives, or other differentials.

basic medical coverage Insurance coverage provided by an organization to its employees whether employer-funded or partially paid by the employees. It typically covers visits to physicians and outpatient clinics for treatment of illnesses and injuries, as well as hospitalization.

basic skills training Traditionally seen as encompassing only reading, writing, and computation, basic skills training is now defined as training provided to upgrade workers' skills, equip them to deal with changes in technology and work processes, and overcome educational deficits.

battery A group of tests that have been validated on the same sample population so that results on the several parts of the battery are comparable. *See also* achievement test.

Beck case A 1988 Supreme Court ruling that established the principle that nonunion workers, who are required to pay dues to organized labor under collective bargaining agreements in 19 states that lack right-to-work laws, can be charged only for activities that directly involve the union's collective bargaining activities. However, the Court failed to specify which nonrelated activities were included or how they should be broken out for accounting purposes. In 1992, the National Labor Relations Board began formulating guidelines for implementing the ruling.

behaviorally anchored rating scale (BARS) An expensive, time-consuming, but extremely effective modification of the **critical incident** approach to rating. Raters are asked to observe and record specific incidents of effective and ineffective performance during a rating period. Those observations are matched against a set of predetermined critical incidents, called a BARS. BARS items are developed as follows: (1) important dimensions of effective performance are identified by workers and supervisors; (2) a second group reviews the incidents to identify effective, average, and ineffective performance; (3) a third group is given the products of the first two groups' efforts and asked to sort the incidents into the dimensions they best represent; (4) a fourth group places a scale value (usually seven or nine points ranging from highly effective to very ineffective) on each incident in each dimension; and (5) the scale is tested by using it with a group of workers, each of whom is rated independently by at least two qualified supervisors.

behavioral objective A training objective that specifies clearly, precisely, and unambiguously what the trainees must *be able to do*, the *conditions* under which they must be able to perform, and the *standard* or *criterion* of acceptable performance, both at critical points during the development of job skills and at the end of the training program.

behavioral psychology or behaviorism A theory of human behavior that holds that the actions of people are determined solely by stimuli (stimulus-response) and that when behavior is reinforced and rewarded that behavior will be repeated, and when ignored or punished, the behavior will be extinguished. That is, human behavior is the result of its consequences whether immediate or delayed.

behavioral simulation A controlled exercise used in screening and selecting candidates for positions in which applicants display directly

observable behaviors relating to selected dimensions of job performance. Examples are planning, selling, and instructing. There are
several types of behavioral simulations: analysis exercises, **in-basket
exercises,** interview simulations, scheduling exercises, and job replica tests.

behavior-based incentive compensation (BBIC) A relatively new and
flexible approach to compensation that uses the power of pay as a
motivator by sharing the benefits of company growth and return on
investment with the employees who made it happen and by tying
compensation to the achievement of stated performance criteria.
BBIC is considered to be a self-funding plan because the gains in
company productivity, service, and profit provide the incentive
compensation budget. *See also* pay for skills.

behavior-based performance appraisal An approach to employee performance appraisal that focuses exclusively on the individual's behavior—that is, what the person *does*—rather than on what he or
she *is like* in terms of personality, traits or characteristics, or skills
and abilities.

benchmarks In job evaluation and compensation, a term used to describe jobs that provide an acceptable basis for interorganizational
comparisons because they occur in several organizational elements,
are reasonably similar in knowledge and skills requirements, and
compare reasonably well with respect to accountability and responsibility. Benchmarks are used to anchor a company's pay scale and
slot other jobs based on their relative worth. *See also* area wage survey; job evaluation; job pricing.

benefits Benefits are economic "goods" granted to employees in addition to base pay. They include financial benefits such as bonuses,
merit salary increases, cost-of-living adjustments, stock ownership
plans, profit-sharing plans, paid holidays, paid vacations, paid sick
leave, paid bereavement leave, group life insurance, group health
insurance, group dental insurance, workers' compensation, unemployment insurance, pension plans, survivor benefits, disability
benefits, maternity leave, child care and elder care, and tuition assistance and reimbursement, whether paid in whole or in part by
the employer. Nonmonetary benefits include flexible work schedules, rest periods and coffee breaks, legal assistance, leaves of ab-
sence, medical examinations and treatment, parking facilities, recreation facilities and programs, travel services and opportunities,
credit and banking services, discounts on products, training and
development, savings plans, and perquisites. Sometimes called
fringe benefits. See also entitlements; equity benefits; protection benefits; statutory benefits.

Bennet Amendment An amendment to the **Equal Pay Act of 1963**, that provides that it is not a violation of the Act for an employer to differentiate (in pay) upon the basis of sex if such differentiation is authorized by the provisions of the Equal Pay Act.

Betts Decision A 1989 Supreme Court Decision (*Public Employees Retirement System of Ohio* v. *Betts*) that says an employer is not required to meet a cost-justification test for benefits; rather, a worker must show that an employee benefit plan was intended to discriminate. In other words, the high court said employee benefit plans do not violate the Age Discrimination in Employment Act of 1967 if they make age-based distinctions.

bidding In employee selection, a means of recruiting that increases the number of internal transfers and promotions, called job bidding. Lists of all current job openings are posted to give current employees the first option to apply for vacant positions. *See also* job posting.

Bloodborne Pathogens Standard An Occupational Health and Safety Administration standard, adopted in December 1991, which requires employers to devise exposure control plans to minimize or eliminate occupational exposure to bloodborne pathogens. The Standard also requires organizations to train all employees, such as workers in laboratories, hospitals, clinics, emergency response units, and physicians' offices, and safety officers, athletic trainers, first-aid providers, and other at-risk employees, who may have occupational exposure to blood, body fluids, and other potentially infectious material. *See also* Confined Spaces Standard; Hazard Communication Standard of 1988; Laboratory Chemical Standard.

bona fide occupational qualification (BFOQ) A legal term used to describe lawfully permissible discriminatory job requirements as an exception to **Title VII** of the Civil Rights Act of 1964. Job applicants may be classified based on BFOQ, which permits employers to discriminate in hiring and promotion only if they have a valid reason directly related to performance of the job. *See also* Mandatory Retirement Age Law of 1978.

bonus After-the-fact, discretionary, extra cash compensation (in addition to base salary) paid to employees based on productivity, profits, savings, cost avoidance, or a combination of two or more of these factors, for a period of 12 months or less.

bonus payment A type of executive incentive plan, whereby bonuses are paid in cash or deferred. *See also* market value plan; self-designed pay plan.

book value plan A type of long-term executive incentive plan in which the company sells its stock to executives at current book value. They receive dividends on the stock and, as the book value increases, the executive's equity also increases. When the executive leaves the company, he or she must sell back the accumulated shares at the current book value. *See also* market value plan; self-designed pay plan.

bootleg contract An agreement between union and management designed to circumvent or evade the union's statutory security limitations.

bounty program An internal recruitment and placement method in which current employees are paid a finder's fee for a referral who is hired by the company.

boutique health care Do-it-yourself health care, paid for by the individual worker. Includes cosmetic surgery.

brainstorming Attributed to Alex Osborn, brainstorming is a freewheeling group ideational technique designed to produce as many ideas as possible within a short period of time. A group of seven to ten, under the direction of a leader, generates ideas using four basic rules: no criticism, freewheeling, quantity, and combination and improvement. Ideas are recorded and subsequently presented to a separate group for evaluation and or use.

brainwriting A group or individual ideational technique, similar to brainstorming. It encourages people to engage in free association to improve their creative thinking abilities and generate new ideas. Ideas are produced by allowing thoughts to be ungoverned, uncontrolled, and unevaluated.

branching program A type of instructional programming that permits trainees to complete training efficiently by skipping whole learning modules (training activities) that represent skills and knowledge already mastered, thereby avoiding duplication or waste of time, and spending more time and effort on modules that represent unknown or unmastered areas of learning.

brand name drug A drug that is sold under a specific trademark name. For example, Inderal is the brand name for propranolol. *See also* formulary drug; generic drug.

bridging pay Severance pay.

broadbanding A compensation strategy used primarily in the public sector to overcome the constraints of a rigid pay structure (general schedule) to meet local market wages. Large numbers of pay grades are merged into a few broad bands of pay.

Brock Commission A commission established by the Secretary of Labor in 1990 to study the skills that young people must master to to have workplace know-how.

bronze parachute Severance packages designed for upper-level managers. Somewhat less lavish than the **golden parachute** received by top executives but more generous than the basic severance plans that cover lower-level employees. In addition, they may be activated by resignation for "good reason" (such as company relocation or change in compensation) as well as by involuntary termination. *See also* tin parachute.

buddy system An executive, management, or supervisor development approach in which a young executive, manager, or supervisor may choose or be assigned a senior executive, manager, or supervisor as a coach and role model.

building block curricula Standard one- or two-week training programs required of employees prior to assignment or promotion to new or more responsible positions. Typically there is a block for first-line supervisors, another for middle managers, and another for executives.

bump/bumping Displacement of an incumbent employee, such as through layoff or demotion, to make room for an employee with seniority or a Title VII litigant—a person who has successfully charged discrimination. Bumping is specifically allowed by the National Labor Relations Board and the Equal Employment Opportunity Commission.

bundled services In-house, complete package (investment management, record keeping, and custody) 401(k) investment services offered employees by companies. *See also* semi-bundled services; unbundled services.

burrowing The practice of getting one's status in the federal bureaucracy changed from political appointee (one who serves at the pleasure of the administration in office) to a bona fide career civil service position (one that cannot be terminated for political reasons).

business necessity Relates to equal employment opportunity. It involves demonstrating that there is an overriding business purpose for any discriminatory practice and that the practice is therefore acceptable. If a practice cannot be defended as a **bona fide occupational qualification**, it is usually justified as a business necessity.

buy right A type of purchasing reform, applied primarily but not exclusively to health care projects, that leans heavily on the use of patient outcome measures as the basis for making buying decisions. Used to select health care providers who can provide the highest quality and most efficient care for the lowest price. Outcome measures include such items as major and minor morbidity and mortality, and patient evaluation of care. The emphasis is on quality, not discounts.

C

CAI	Computer-aided instruction.
CAJE	Computer-assisted job evaluation.
CAP	Closing Agreement Program.
CCR&R	Child care resource and referral program.
CD	Career development.
CERCLA	Comprehensive Environmental Response, Compensation, and Liability Act of 1980.
CEU	Continuing Education Unit.
CMI	Computer-managed instruction.
CMO	Case management organization.
CMP	Competitive medical plan.
COBRA	Consolidated Omnibus Budget Reconciliation Act of 1986.
CODA	Cash or deferred arrangement.
COLI	Corporate-owned life insurance.
COP	Continuation of pay.
CORF	Comprehensive outpatient rehabilitation facility.
CPT	Common procedural terminology.
CRA	Civil Rights Acts of 1964 and 1968.
CWHSSA	Contract Work Hours and Safety Standards Act of 1962.

cafeteria plan An employee benefit plan that allows employees to select from an array of benefits, within a specified dollar limit, those that most closely match their requirements, and to choose the form in which incentive payments are to be received. Usually a common core of benefits is required, such as minimum levels of disability, health, retirement, and death benefits. *See also* flexible benefits/flex benefits program; Section 125, Internal Revenue Code.

call-back pay Guaranteed pay for a minimum number of hours when employees are called back to the workplace at a time when they are not scheduled.

call-in pay Guaranteed pay for a minimum number of hours when an employee reports to the workplace and there is no work.

capital accumulation plan A long-term benefits plan designed to motivate and reward management and encourage employees to save a portion of their income for a time when they will need it to meet capital needs or for supplemental retirement income. *See also* phantom stock plan, profit-sharing plan; thrift savings plan.

captives A strategy to reduce the costs of liability insurance coverage (and sometimes workers' compensation). Captives involve the creation of group insurance companies by corporations. They are industry-supported insurance ventures or insurance companies owned by a group of competing organizations in an industry. They may also share cost-control ideas, manage claims and reserves, and generate return-on-investment premiums.

career audit An annual, semiannual, or quarterly review of career plans and progress. It is a management strategy to help an individual look at the realities of his or her work life. It helps employees examine why they do what they do, how to take responsibility for their own careers, and how to identify the resources they need to manage a career in a changing environment.

career counseling Helping employees learn about their own capabilities, assets, limitations, preferences, and objectives, where they stand in the organization, what opportunities are available to them within and outside the organization, and what they need in the way of training and development to employ their talents and make the most of their opportunities. Then, employees are assisted in developing individual career plans, using information on specific career requirements, career ladders, organizational needs, available development opportunities, and employee interests and needs. *See also* developmental counseling.

career development (CD) The process of assessing, aligning, and balancing organizational and individual needs, capabilities, opportunities, and challenges through multiple approaches and methods. It emphasizes the person as an individual who performs, configures, and adapts various work roles. Its major intervention is self-assessment and development processes that affect individual and organizational abilities to generate optimal matches of people to jobs. *See also* development.

career ladder A carefully sequenced series of jobs from the lowest to the highest level (in terms of responsibilities, compensation, and challenges) in a career field available in an organization. It marks a clear path for development and promotion. Also called *career path*. *See also* progression chart.

career management profile A means of storing and communicating data about an individual employee; for example, appraisal of performance and potential, training and development needs, and primary and alternate career paths.

career planning The process of establishing short- or long-term career goals and objectives and defining the specific steps required to achieve them (the positions, training, development, and other experiences that will assist in attaining the goals and objectives). It may be done by the employee alone or in concert with a mentor or advisor.

carrel An individual learning environment typically found in learning centers. One carrel consists of a partitioned area containing a desk and chair, a computer terminal or personal computer and associated disk drive, cables, telephone, modem, or other devices, and audio, visual, and other materials in document form.

carve-outs A means of cutting medical and health care costs, particularly mental health care, substance abuse benefits, chiropractic and physical therapy claims, diagnostic testing services, and drug utilization. Similar to managed care strategies, such as **health maintenance organizations** and **preferred provider organizations**, but carve-outs emphasize precertification, utilization review, and case management in specific areas of medical treatment that require more intensive and specialized approaches.

case management A program that has its origins in workers' compensation and long-term disability rehabilitation. Designed to facilitate cost-effective treatment and care and an optimum level of recovery for injured or ill employees. The goal is to identify and coordinate all the resources needed to offer quality options to the patient and maximize the effectiveness of the health care provided. There are three steps in the process: (1) diagnosis and assessment; (2) planning and coordinating therapy; and (3) monitoring treatment. The process involves the patient, the attending medical professional, the family, and a case manager.

case management organization (CMO) A health care management organization that reviews medical products and services to help corporations determine their therapeutic value and cost-effectiveness.

cash account pension plan *See* cash balance pension plan.

cash balance pension plan A defined benefit plan. Provides a career average means of calculating pension benefits. The annuity at retirement is based on earnings of a phantom investment account that must be credited periodically at current market rates. Those calculations give plan participants an estimate of their accrued benefits on a defined contribution equivalent basis. *See also* defined benefit pension plan; life cycle pension plan.

cash-deferred [401(k)] plan A savings plan under which employees are given the options of either deferring part of their income to be invested in a group plan or receiving that same amount in cash on a current basis. Originally, the deferred amount and accumulated interest and dividends could be completely sheltered from current taxation. The deferred amount was considered a reduction in salary and constituted a reduction in the individual's gross taxable income. However, in 1989 Congress tightened its control by including 401(k) contributions in the measurement of taxes due under the **Federal Insurance Contributions Act of 1935**.

cash or deferred arrangement (CODA) *See* cash-deferred [401(k)] plan.

cash plan A type of profit-sharing plan in which a certain percentage of the profits is distributed in cash at predetermined times to participants in the plan. *See also* Lincoln incentive system.

change model A form of statistical HR forecasting approach that assesses the impact of past employment practices and tries to project future human resource availability given certain assumptions about organizational change.

chargeback A system for funding training that involves charging back or "billing" the trainee's department for costs incurred by the training department—instructor's fees, training materials, overhead costs, and so on. It can affect positively the way corporations and line managers perceive the value of training and development.

charm school A derisive or mocking term applied by cynics to military instructor training courses and civilian train-the-trainer programs.

check-off Deduction of union dues or assessments from an employee's pay for transfer to the union.

cherry picking The insurance industry's version of **adverse selection**, a form of discrimination. To reduce claims, the insurance company writes policies that exclude persons with preexisting conditions and experience-rates the coverage to eliminate high-risk individuals, companies, and industries. *See also* risk rating.

child care A relatively new employee benefit; providing day care facilities and personnel either on-site or near-site to care for the children of employees, or providing full or partial reimbursement for such care. *See also* elder care.

child care resource and referral program (CCR&R) Services provided to employees through in-house sources or by contract with a community-based resource and referral agency. They may inform employees about the different forms of child care available in the community, identify the ones that have vacancies, provide detailed information about each service, help parents choose the best arrangement for their child, help new child care programs get started, and speak out on child care issues.

child-labor law Under federal law, 14- and 15-year-olds are allowed to work only three hours per day and a maximum of 18 hours per week when school is in session and only between the hours of 6 a.m. and 7 p.m. They may work longer hours on weekends and during the summer.

Civil Rights Act of 1964 (CRA) Title VII of the Act prohibits discrimination in hiring, firing, promotion, compensation and other terms, privileges, and conditions of employment and facilities on the basis of an employee's race, color, religion, sex, or national origin. Provisions relate to application forms and photographs, help-wanted ads, interviews, physical examinations, formal tests, and assessment centers. The Act applies to state and local governments and all public and private organizations engaged in interstate commerce, including employment agencies and labor unions with at least 15 employees. The Act also established the Equal Employment Opportunity Commission (EEOC). The EEOC issued the EEOC **Uniform Guidelines on Employee Selection Procedures**. A 1992 amendment (Section 705) created a revolving fund within the EEOC which allows it to charge employers and individuals reasonable fees for some of its services to offset the costs of new services, such as developing training programs and producing videos. *See also* affirmative action plan; equal employment opportunity; Equal Employment Opportunity Act of 1972; fetal risk.

Civil Rights Act of 1968 (CRA) Identifies federally protected activities. Among them are willful injury, intimidation, or interference by anyone on account of race, color, religion, or national origin to dissuade or prevent participation in any benefit, service, privilege, program, facility, or activity provided or administered by the U.S. government, including applying for or enjoying employment by any agency of the federal government or enrolling in any public school or public college. The Act also establishes penalties for violators.

Civil Rights Act of 1991 Section 106 of the Act, which became effective November 26, 1991, states, "It shall be an unlawful employment practice for a respondent, in connection with the selection or referral of applicants or candidates for employment or promotion, to adjust the scores of, use different cutoff scores for, or otherwise alter the results of, employment related tests on the basis of race, color, religion, sex, or national origin." In effect, the Act placed the burden of proof on employers to show that there is a business necessity for their tests. *See also* Civil Rights and Women's Equity in Employment Act of 1991.

Civil Rights and Women's Equity in Employment Act of 1991 Partially offsets seven Supreme Court decisions that made it more difficult for victims (women and religious minorities) of employment discrimination, including the disabled, to sue and collect damages for job discrimination. In addition to lawsuits for discrimination in promotion and dismissal, the Act permits victims of intentional sexual discrimination, including sexual harassment, to seek compensatory and punitive damages, up to fixed limits (ranging from $50,000 for companies with between 15 and 100 employees and up to $300,000 for organizations with more than 500 employees). Employers are now required to demonstrate that their allegedly discriminatory practices are job-related and consistent with business necessity. The bill (1) allows plaintiffs who litigate intentional discrimination claims under **Title VII** to have their claims heard by a jury and, if successful, to recover compensatory and punitive damages; (2) requires companies to establish the **business necessity** of any employment practice deemed to have a **disparate impact** on members of a **protected class**; (3) provides that when an employee's race, color, religion, sex, or national origin is a "contributing factor" to an employment decision, that decision is unlawful; (4) ensures that seniority systems developed through collective bargaining agreements, which have the intent of discriminating against a protected class, may be challenged throughout the period that the pact remains in effect; (5) shortens the time during which an employee may challenge any employment practice that follows an earlier **consent decree** or order which resolved an employment discrimination claim under federal statute; and (6) expands the period for filing discrimination charges with the **EEOC** from 180 days to two years. The bill also encourages **alternative dispute resolution procedures** (such as mediation and arbitration) to avert jury trials. The Act also made it easier to sue for age bias at work by repealing the 2-year statute of limitations for filing job-discrimination lawsuits under the federal **Age Discrimination in Employment Act of 1967**. Plaintiffs may now go into court at any time following the filing of charges with the Equal Employment Opportunity Commission.

claims substantiation Written benefits statements required by an employer or insurer from a qualified and independent third party stating the date, and type and amount of medical service provided by a health care professional or facility and affirming that those services were not reimbursed by another health care plan.

climate survey A variant of the attitude and opinion survey, a climate survey attempts to measure employee attitudes toward factors considered important in establishing the climate of an organization: clarity of goals and standards, working relationships, opportunities for personal development, management's credibility, degree of authority and responsibility, and so on. *See also* organization climate survey.

clock hour A measure of instructor work load and student course load and a means of converting time to credit hours in colleges, universities, and technical schools. One clock hour is a minimum of 50 minutes of instruction, including breaks. *See also* credit hour.

closed pay system A pay system in which the amount of pay employees receive is kept secret. Theoretically, no employee knows what his or her fellow workers are being paid. *See also* open pay system; pay secrecy.

closed shop A union security measure that requires a company to hire only union members. It was outlawed in 1947 but still remains in a few industries. *See also* agency shop; maintenance of membership; open shop; union shop.

Closing Agreement Program (CAP) An Internal Revenue Service enforcement vehicle for qualified pension plans initiated in 1990. The plan allows employers to avoid plan disqualification by remedying certain types of violations and paying a fine. The program enabled employers to talk to the IRS anonymously and negotiate fines without risk. Also called *John Doe cases*.

coaching A one-on-one, face-to-face teaching/learning/counseling relationship designed to develop job-related knowledge and skills and improve performance. Involves a continuous flow of instructions, comments, and suggestions from coach to employee—listening, questioning, relating learning to the learner's experiences, and providing guided practice. Also called *tutoring*.

code gaming Insurance rip-offs, some bordering on fraud, by unscrupulous physicians and other health care providers to maintain incomes that have been eroded by the increasing costs of of operating a medical or related practice, such as malpractice insurance and laws against balance billing. The most common are upcoding, unbundling, and **exploding**.

cognitive domain 1. Applied to human learning, the area of learning that is represented by facts, knowledge, and skills, rather than feelings. 2. A classification of instructional objectives that deals with the recall or recognition of knowledge and the development of mental skills and abilities. *See also* affective domain; psychomotor domain.

coinsurance In employee benefits, a cost-sharing requirement that provides that a beneficiary will assume a portion or percentage of the reasonable and customary costs of covered medical or other health care services, usually after paying the deductible.

collaborative appraisal Cooperative appraisal or evaluation of performance involving both the manager and the employee. They jointly establish the standards, choose the performance measures, evaluate progress and accomplishment, identify needed improvements, and establish an action plan.

collective bargaining Good faith negotiations conducted between a union and a firm to reach an agreement or contract regarding work-related issues and problems such as pay, benefits, hours, working conditions, and the like and the execution of a written contract incorporating agreements reached if requested by either party. *See also* labor-management contract.

common procedural terminology (CPT) Codes approved by the American Medical Association for use in identifying common medical procedures in automated systems for handling insurance claims.

compact A partnership or alliance among businesses, educational institutions, and municipal governments to achieve such goals as improved educational opportunity, higher educational standards, reduction in the school dropout rate, increased attendance, and helping high school and college students get summer jobs, part-time jobs while in school, and full-time jobs following graduation.

comparable factors *See* compensable factors.

comparable worth Applies to job evaluation and the administration of compensation programs. It is a concept and a strategy designed to overcome the male-female salary gap and the pay inequities caused by what have traditionally been female jobs. It promotes the concept of "equal pay for work of equal worth." Male and female jobs, including dissimilar jobs, are compared and matched in terms of difficulty and requirements (skill, effort, and responsibility), and matching salaries are established for the female jobs. *See also* Equal Pay Act of 1963.

compa-ratio The relationship, expressed as a percent, of actual salaries to the midpoint of the salary range established for a job within the salary grade structure. For example, if an employee in Grade 9 has a salary of $32,000 and the Grade 9 midpoint is $36,000, the employee has a compa-ratio of 88.9 percent ($32,000 divided by $36,000).

comparative ratings An approach to rating that compares people; that is, each person is rated only in comparison with others. Examples, are rank order, equal intervals, paired comparisons, and forced distribution rating methods.

compbusters Measures taken to eliminate or reduce the incidence of employee accidents, injuries, or other sources of claims for compensation.

compelled self-defamation A legal tort that holds employers liable for giving a false or incorrect reason to an employee for his or her termination, knowing that the employee will have to pass the reason on to a prospective employer.

compensable factors In job evaluation, the basic criteria used to determine the relative worth of jobs. They consist of the attributes which, in the judgment of management, constitute the basis for establishing relative worth; for example, knowledge, skills, training, experience, accountability, responsibility, working conditions, and so on. *See also* factor comparison; job classification; job evaluation; job ranking; wage curve.

compensation Remuneration for work performed or services rendered in the form of pay and allowances, salaries, wages, stipends, fees and commissions, and bonuses and stock options.

compensatory time Time off the job and away from the workplace earned by workers by working overtime, on weekends or holidays, or during scheduled vacations. Usually limited to exempt employees; nonexempt workers are paid overtime wages.

compensatory training Training provided to remedy worker deficiencies in knowledge and skills. Includes basic skills training, remedial training, and retraining.

competence A social concept involving a comparative judgment about the value or worth of human performance. It is comparative in that it compares typical performance with exemplary performance.

competency assessment In selection for employment or promotion, evaluation of potential based on appraisal of skills and abilities.

competency-based test In selection and training, a test that measures specific skills or competencies, rather than job knowledge. *See also* criterion-referenced test; performance test.

competency-based training Training that is rooted in the skills and competencies required for acceptable job performance as determined by job and task analysis. *See also* embedded training.

competitive medical plan (CMP) A prepayment health care plan requiring fixed monthly payments and minimal copayments. CMPs with corporate or Medicare contracts offer beneficiaries all services covered by fee-for-service Medicare or other private plans. *See also* health maintenance organization.

composite score A single score that combines several scores, usually simply by summing them, but sometimes weights are assigned to the separate scores to increase or decrease their importance in the total composite score.

Comprehensive Environmental Response, Compensation, and Liability Act (CERCLA) of 1980 One of five major environmental laws since significantly revised, expanded, and extended. The Act identifies 717 hazardous substances. *See also* Hazard Communication Standard of 1988; Superfund Amendments and Reauthorization Act of 1986.

comprehensive medical coverage Medical insurance plans that cover hospitalization and the fees of medical and surgical practitioners. Often includes prescription drugs.

comprehensive outpatient rehabilitation facility (CORF) A health care facility that provides speech, occupational, and respiratory therapies and counseling and related services.

compressed workweek A scheduling plan that allows employees to rearrange their work hours to help balance work and family responsibilities. For example, the 40-hour workweek could be compressed into four 10-hour workdays, or a fortnightly schedule may be used to allow workers one additional day off every two weeks. *See also* flexible work options; flexiplace.

compression In wage and salary administration, pay differentials between classes of workers (supervisors and workers, new hires and experienced workers, and job grades, for example) that are too small to be fair and equitable.

comp self-insurance An alternate way of financing coverage for workers' compensation claims. Employers band together in self-insurance groups that operate somewhat like risk pools. Objectives include having funding at least match claims payments and building surpluses that can be returned to the employers.

computer-aided instruction (CAI) Training that involves the use of computers to conduct, or assist in conducting, instruction. It involves software and **learningware** that permit the individual learner to proceed at his or her own pace through an instructional sequence or package. Sometimes linked to video or other media, including written documentation. Also called *computer-assisted training* and *computer-based training*.

computer-assisted job evaluation (CAJE) An alternative to the traditional point-factor method of job evaluation claimed by some to be capable of automatically producing a job description, a job evaluation, and a quality assurance report on the accuracy of a job analysis. At the very least, the computer-driven system speeds up the job evaluation process, but the ultimate accuracy of the system depends on the appropriateness and quality of the input and the techniques used to establish the standards.

computer-based coaching Use of a computer as a job aid. The aid is controlled by the workers—that is, they initiate it and decide when they don't need it, based on their performance of job tasks.

computer-managed instruction (CMI) The use of a computer to manage instructional systems and programs. It performs such time-consuming tasks as testing trainees and tracking and recording their progress and accomplishment; developing and implementing training prescriptions tailored to the needs of individual trainees; maintaining inventories and records pertaining to trainees, training space, facilities, equipment, materials, and supplies; and performing other resource allocation, accounting, and reporting functions. CMI employs a computer with its associated hardware, software, and **learningware**.

conciliation A formal request to "conciliate" (reconcile) made by the Equal Employment Opportunity Commission when it issues a "cause" finding (reason to believe that discrimination has taken place) following a **fact-finding conference** to investigate a charge of discrimination.

concurrent validity 1. A training program or test has concurrent validity when performance of trainees or testees correlates highly with other measures of job performance. **2.** In test construction, the practice of comparing the test scores of employees with their current performance as a means of verifying the validity of a test. The approach is questionable because current employees may not be representative of new applicants for positions. *See also* content validity.

conditions of employment Organizational policies and work rules that apply to employees; for example, probationary periods, absences, tardiness, rest periods, vacations, overtime, suspensions, layoffs, dismissals, and such special circumstances as bereavement, pregnancy, childbirth or adoption, and accommodation for religious observances. Such conditions must be clearly defined, codified, and communicated to all concerned.

conduit IRA *See* rollover.

confidentiality agreement An agreement signed by an employee stipulating that he or she will not disclose company plans, designs, financial position, or other proprietary matters either during employment with the firm or following termination for any reason. *See also* disclosure agreement.

Confined Spaces Standard Rules established by the Occupational Safety and Health Administration pertaining to the identification of "confined spaces" and the protection of employees from safety hazards arising from the use of those spaces. Those spaces are defined as areas not intended for employee occupancy, such as storage tanks, boilers, silos, and process vessels, which could have inadequate ventilation, hazardous atmospheres because of toxic fumes, or limited means of entrance or exit. The standards became effective in February 1992. *See also* Bloodborne Pathogens Standard; Hazard Communication Standard of 1988; Laboratory Chemical Standard.

consent decree An agreement reached between two disputants to resolve a claim of some kind; for example, an employment discrimination claim.

consent form A form used by employers to obtain written consent from employees for specified actions or practices. *See also* Retirement Equity Act of 1984.

Consolidated Omnibus Budget Reconciliation Act of 1986 (COBRA) A comprehensive federal law with many provisions covering employee benefit plans. It applies to employers of 20 or more workers. COBRA mandated continuation of group health care insurance plans for up to 36 months, at workers' expense, after they leave the company, their work hours are reduced, or they die, divorce, legally separate, or their dependents **age out**. COBRA has been modified by virtually every comprehensive budget and tax law since its enactment. Effective January 1, 1990, Congress extended COBRA coverage to 29 months (up from 18 months) for disabled employees who receive Social Security benefits. That measure included a provision requiring companies to offer continuation COBRA coverage to former employees until after their new employer's plan covers preexisting conditions. Other changes relate to new rules on Medicare as a qualifying event; multiemployer plans; controlled groups; self-employed individuals, partners, and outside directors, and other service providers; and partner-only plans. These changes make it necessary for employers to modify existing COBRA forms and systems and may require reexamination of claims refused under the 1989 rules. Recent court decisions, new regulations and changes to the law: (1) An employer cannot drop COBRA as soon as a former employee is covered by another employer's health plan if the new employer's coverage contains a preexisting condition provision. (2) The spouse and dependents of an employee on COBRA who become entitled to Medicare can elect 36 months of coverage starting on the Medicare entitlement date. *See also* conversion insurance.

consortium child care center A dependent care facility where the costs and responsibilities are shared by several employers, sometimes together with a community agency and/or a union. The consortium may form a not-for-profit corporation to fund a day care center located in downtown areas or in office parks convenient to all businesses contributing to the consortium. *See also* family day care network.

construct validity **1.** In assessment centers and in other instruments and strategies used in selection, promotion, and evaluation, the requirement that the knowledge, skills, or other dimensions of performance to be measured are relevant to job performance. **2.** In tests, the extent to which a test measures some relatively abstract psychological trait. It is used to judge the appropriateness of personality, verbal ability, and mechanical aptitude tests. *See also* content validity; criterion validity.

contact hours A measure of instructor work load. The number of hours per week that an instructor is in direct contact with students in a classroom, laboratory, or other learning environment. *See also* credit hour.

content validity Applies to selection, training, and testing. A selection strategy, training program, or test has content validity if it samples adequately from actual job content; that is, if selection mechanisms, training objectives, and test items require performance or simulated performance of real job duties and tasks and the testing procedure requires behaviors and conditions similar to those required on the job. *See also* concurrent validity; construct validity; criterion validity.

context evaluation Assessment of the job environment, including the attitudes of managers and workers toward training and development. *See also* impact evaluation.

contingent annuity In benefits, an annuity that is payable to the annuitant until his or her death, at which point it becomes payable, in whole or in part, to a named survivor until his or her death.

contingent work force Part-time, temporary, contract, and various types of free-lance workers. Typically they receive low pay, few benefits, and enjoy little or no job security. A cost-saving strategy adopted by more and more organizations. As of 1992, numbered about 30 million workers—one in four in the United States. Also called *disposable workers*. *See also* sheddable worker.

continuation of pay (COP) Regular compensation (with the usual deductions for taxes, insurance, and so on) paid to employees who have suffered on-the-job injuries. Also applies to compensation paid to employees for a set period of time following layoff or retirement.

continued care Health care benefits provided when a subscriber or employee has a lengthy illness or long recovery period. Typically provided in skilled nursing facilities, chronic disease hospitals, noncustodial nursing homes, home health care, or hospice care.

continuing education Programs of education and training offered by private and public educational institutions, professional and technical organizations and associations, and private and public businesses to upgrade the knowledge and skills of adult learners or to enhance and improve their general level of education.

continuing education unit (CEU) A measure of nondegree credit awarded to participants in training programs by professional associations, educational institutions, and some private firms upon completion of courses, seminars, or workshops. One CEU equals 10 hours of participation in an organized educational experience under the sponsorship and direction of a qualified training organization.

contract administration The system by which a labor-management contract or collective bargaining agreement is administered on a day-to-day basis; for example, following the filing of a grievance, whether or not a contract provision has been violated.

contract training Use of outside sources (either on-site or off the premises) to provide training programs for operative, supervisory, or managerial personnel. Sources include colleges and universities, professional societies, management institutes and associations, and management and training companies and consultants.

Contract Work Hours and Safety Standards Act of 1962 (CWHSSA) An Act mandating that the wages of every laborer and mechanic employed by any contractor or subcontractor of government (U.S. agency, District of Columbia, or territory) public works contracts, or for work financed in whole or in part by loans or grants by the federal government, be computed on the basis of a standard workweek of 40 hours and that a rate not less than one and one-half times the basic rate of pay be paid for all hours worked in excess of the 40-hour workweek. The Act further states that no contractor or subcontractor shall require any laborer or mechanic to work in surroundings or under working conditions that are unsanitary, hazardous, or dangerous to health and safety.

contributory benefits plan Benefits plan in which employees contribute part or all of the cost of benefits, with the employer covering the remainder of the costs, if any.

conversion insurance Coverage that gives former employees whose health insurance coverage under the **Consolidated Omnibus Budget Reconciliation Act of 1986** (COBRA) has run out or who can't get health insurance elsewhere the opportunity to buy coverage. It is more expensive than COBRA coverage, requires higher deductibles and copayments, has low lifetime limits, and doesn't include ancillary coverage (such as treatment for substance abuse). It is most often purchased by people who are between jobs (short-termers) and those who have chronic illnesses or are older but under age 65 and therefore not eligible for Medicare (long-termers).

cooperative education Partnerships between businesses, industrial firms, or professional organizations and educational institutions to provide internships or firsthand experience, with college credit and pay, for college or university students engaged in studies relating to the business, industry, or profession.

coordinated care plan *See* managed care.

coordination of benefits Refers to provisions in a benefits plan designed to prevent double payments when an employee is covered by two health care plans. The primary plan reimburses the individual or the provider first, up to the limits of the plan, and the benefits of the secondary plan are adjusted so that the total amount does not exceed the cost of covered services. *See also* maintenance of benefits; Medicare carve-out.

copayment Refers to patient (employee) out-of-pocket expenses for health care. May be a percentage of the Medicare- or company-approved charge or a flat dollar amount. Also called *coinsurance*.

core curriculum Training specifically designed and provided for people at each of several levels in an organization. Typically, there is a central theme and the only change lies in the scope and complexity of the content and the problems dealt with at each level.

core work activities The tasks that must be performed if an organization is to fulfill its mission and achieve its goals and objectives.

core workers Permanent employees who are important to the survival and competitiveness of a business or industry. They are considered to be indispensable. *See also* temporary employees.

corporate-owned life insurance (COLI) A means of funding postretirement medical and death benefits limited by Congress to executive employees. Consists of insurance policies on the life of key executives in which the corporation is the beneficiary. The corporation is the owner and beneficiary of the policies and holds all ownership rights, including the right to death benefits and cash value. Employees have no rights to the policies; however, if the insured dies while coverage is in effect, the firm may make an equivalent noninsured payment to the designated survivor(s). In any case, the corporation receives the policy proceeds on a tax-free basis and uses them to fund the benefits or reimburse the corporation for benefits already paid. Beginning in 1992, the Financial Standards Accounting Board required employers to include postretirement benefits on their balance sheets.

cost containment lump-sum payment A one-time bonus given to employees for performance above a stated level. It does not become a part of the employee's salary.

cost per applied person-day A worker's full cost per day divided by his or her applied rate.

cost-per-hire A basic element of the employee recruitment budget usually categorized by exempt and nonexempt jobs and often by job category. Sometimes used to measure the effectiveness of the recruitment department and individual recruiters. Cost includes such elements as advertising, applicant travel and subsistence, recruiter travel and subsistence, employment agency or search fees, and new employee relocation.

cost sharing A strategy to contain health care costs and the costs of other benefits by giving employees more of the responsibility for their own retirement and health care planning and financing. Examples of legislation that has passed responsibility to the individual and the employer include Medicare Benefits Cost-Sharing, Financial Accounting Standards Board Retiree Accounting Rules, Social Security tax, and the **Consolidated Omnibus Budget Reconciliation Act of 1986**.

cost-shifting In benefits, cost reduction strategies designed to transfer more of the costs of providing health care from the organization to employees. It is accomplished by (1) higher deductibles and employee copayments and contributions, (2) use of the **Consolidated Omnibus Budget Reconciliation Act of 1986** to shift costs to other firms when the employee moves to a new employer, and (3) getting employees to opt for managed care programs (health maintenance organizations and preferred provider organizations) with strong **utilization review**.

country executive program A program designed to assist in corporate globalization. Top officers (usually divisional presidents) choose or are assigned a country or area of the world and make themselves responsible for learning its history, politics, culture, and sometimes language through training, individual study, and frequent trips to the country or area. They are often responsible for overseeing visits to the corporate office in the United States by natives of the designated country and act as senior business "diplomats."

courseware Software produced for use with computer-based training systems; the programs used for presenting the course content along with the books, film, video, and audio materials that support the training. *See also* learningware.

covered care Health care services covered by an insurance policy. It typically requires that services be provided by a licensed physician or nurse, a licensed physical, occupational, or speech therapist, other licensed health care provider, home health care agency-furnished home health aide or personal care attendant, or day care services received at an adult day care center.

covered employee A worker protected by (nonexempt from) the provisions of employment laws. For example, under the Omnibus Budget Reconciliation Act of 1989, the term "covered employees" now includes independent contractors, partners, and self-employed individuals covered under a group health plan.

credit hour A measure of instructor work load and student course load and a means of converting time to credit in colleges, universities, and technical schools. One semester hour of credit is generally awarded for each block of 15 clock hours of lecture, 30 clock hours of laboratory, or 45 clock hours of externship/clinical instruction. One quarter-hour of credit is usually awarded for each 10 clock hours of laboratory or 30 clock hours of externship/clinical instruction. *See also* clock hour.

criterion measure A means of evaluating the adequacy and effectiveness of an instructional system. A test constructed to measure achievement of required knowledge supports and mastery of essential skills at the task or duty level of job performance. *See also* job performance measure; performance test.

criterion-referenced test A test that is relevant to real-world job requirements; a performance test that focuses on the duties and tasks of a job. *See also* competency-based test.

criterion validity Applies to training and testing. There are two types: criterion concurrent validity and criterion predictive validity. A training program or test has criterion concurrent validity when selection instrument scores or criterion test scores correlate highly with measures of job performance. It has criterion predictive validity when measures of actual on-the-job performance correlate highly with selection instrument scores or criterion test scores during or at the end of training. *See also* construct validity; content validity.

critical incident 1. In training needs analysis, an analytical tool that involves collecting statements based on direct observation of job incumbents by supervisors or designated observers or recall of job behavior by employees that typify both competent and incompetent performance of a job or task. The technique underscores critical job behaviors for emphasis in training and the supervision of workplace performance. 2. In performance rating, a descriptive approach in which the rater is asked to observe and record specific incidents of effective and ineffective performance during a rating period. The observations are matched against a predetermined critical incident, often referred to as a behaviorally anchored rating scale. The incidents are discussed with the employee and are used as a basis for developing an improvement plan.

critical pathway A health care management tool pioneered by a coalition of six Chicago hospitals to reduce costs and improve the quality of care of cardiac cases. The pathway is a planned progression controlled by standard physician orders for diagnostic tests and medication and anticipated activities and treatments for each day of hospitalization, from admission through discharge. The plan will also be used to track variations and, when treatment departs from the path, the reason is recorded. Over time it is anticipated that variations can be linked to outcomes and cost. If successful, the concept may be applied to other types of cases such as mental health/chemical dependency.

cross-cultural training Training provided by multinational or multicultural organizations, public and private institutions and agencies, and the military services to increase managerial effectiveness in domestic cross-cultural settings and international operations, negotiations, and decision making, help employees adapt to working, living, and learning environments in cultural settings that differ from their own, establish and maintain friendly, cooperative, and favorable relationships with the people of the host country, and assist HR personnel to adapt training objectives, strategies, methods, and materials to the people of the cultures they are charged to train or develop. *See also* intercultural training.

cross-training A means of developing multiskilled workers, people who can adapt to changes in job requirements and advancing technology. Cross training is essentially a strategy to make an organization more competitive, increase productivity, promote stability, respond more rapidly to change, avoid layoffs, and compensate for the shrinking pool of qualified workers. It is accomplished by such means as conventional training, on-the-job training, and peer training. Sometimes called *upskilling* or *redeployment*.

cross validation In test construction, the practice of administering the test to additional groups of subjects to recheck the findings of the first validation study; that is, determine whether there is a significant relationship (correlation) between scores (the predictor) and performance (the criterion). Sometimes called *revalidation*.

customary charge The amount that physicians or medical suppliers most frequently charge for each separate service and supply furnished. This charge is the usually the maximum amount a health insurance plan will allow for covered expenses.

customer rating (appraisal) system Tapping customers or clients for appraisal data on employees such as salespersons, repair specialists, consultants, and the like.

custom training program A training program designed specifically for a particular group of people in a specific organization. Employs problems, situations, and other content unique to the target group.

D

DAA	Deposit administration arrangement.
DBA	Davis-Bacon Acts of 1931 and 1964.
DBP	Defined benefit plan.
DCAP	Dependent care assistance plan.
DCM	Disability case management.
DCP	1. Defined contribution plan. 2. Dental capitation plan. 3. Dental care plan. 4. Dependent care program.
DCR	Dependent-care reimbursement.
DCW	Dependent coverage waiver.
DDS	Disability Determination Service.
DEFRA	Deficit Reduction Act of 1984.
DFWA	Drug-Free Workplace Act of 1988.
DOMO	Downwardly mobile professional.
DPPO	Dental preferred provider organization.
DRGs	Diagnosis-related groups.
DUR	Drug utilization review.

daddy track The career path taken by male employees who give priority to their families when making career plans. Such workers often demand more job flexibility and invariably place family obligations and considerations ahead of everything, including opportunities for promotion. *See also* grandpa track; mommy track.

daily maximum The largest amount that a health care insurance policy will pay for care (other than for covered equipment purchases) that a beneficiary receives for any one calendar day of confinement to a health care facility. *See also* maximum payment period.

daily work record A method of job analysis. Job incumbents are required to fill out daily records of tasks performed over a period of weeks or months. Reports are tabulated and analyzed to identify tasks performed by workers. Results are used to prepare job descriptions and performance standards, and as a basis for training programs.

Davis-Bacon Acts of 1931 and 1964 (DBA) Require most federal contractors, employers in construction, and those in related areas to pay prevailing wage rates. Amendments provide for employee fringe benefits and mandate records retention requirements. The Acts apply to employers on contracts exceeding $2,000. *See also* McNamara-O'Hara Service Contract Act of 1965; prevailing wage rate.

day care reimbursement account Payments to employees for day care expenses that are nontaxable if certain rules are met: (1) the annual amount reimbursed must be less than the lower of the employee's or spouse's income; (2) the payment must be for the care of a dependent who is under the age of 13 or who is physically or mentally incapable of self-care; (3) payments cannot be made to a person who is claimed as the employee's dependent on his or her income tax return; (4) when care is provided by a dependent care center or in an individual's home that provides for more than six individuals, the center or home must comply with all state and local laws; and (5) the person providing care must sign the reimbursement claim form or provide an invoice or receipt that includes his or her Social Security or care center license number. *See also* health care reimbursement account; reimbursement account.

deauthorization *See* deunionization.

decertification *See* deunionization.

dedicated defined contribution plan account A plan for meeting retiree medical liabilities in which benefits are funded by using a portion of profit-sharing accounts to purchase insurance coverage or reimburse annuitants for medical expenses.

deferred annuity An annuity that provides that the money invested in the contract be held by the insurer until some future time (such as the normal retirement age), at which time payments to the beneficiary will begin. In the intervening time, investment earnings are credited to the contract. *See also* group annuity.

deferred arrangement *See* Section 401(k), Internal Revenue Code.

deferred benefits plan A retirement plan designed as an incentive for employees to remain with an organization for a full career. It prefunds and guarantees the benefits an employee will receive in retirement. Typically the employer calculates the benefits based on average annual income during the employee's last three to five years of service. Usually a minimum period of employment is required to vest in the plan. *See also* equity benefits.

deferred compensation 1. In general, any compensation payments that accrue to an employee at some time in the future (such as pension fund annuities) and are sheltered from taxation until paid. **2.** A form of economic reward for outstanding performance or accomplishments (usually executives). The company invests a specified amount of money each year for a specific period of time in a mutual fund or other investment in the name and ownership of the corporation. Each year, the corporation borrows a certain percentage against the collateral of this investment to buy a cash-value life insurance policy on the life of the insured; the policy is owned by the employee. Upon retirement, the executive or his or her beneficiary receives an annual percentage of the net value of the investment at the time of retirement. The executive gets additional current compensation, a substantial life insurance policy against which he or she can borrow, and deferred compensation at retirement. *See also* equity benefits; incentive plan.

deferred profit-sharing plan A type of pension plan in which a portion of a company's profits are credited to each employee's account, placed under the supervision of a trustee, and distributed to the employee or his or her beneficiaries upon retirement or death. There are no guaranteed benefits. *See also* defined contribution plan; group pension plan; savings and thrift plan.

Deficit Reduction Act of 1984 (DEFRA) Federal legislation that proscribes inclusion of taxable benefits as part of a flexible benefits plan. It also requires employers to give employees' spouses age 65 or older the option of enrolling in group health insurance benefits plans as an alternative to Medicare. Added new sections (419 and 419A) to the Internal Revenue Code limit the deductibility of contributions to welfare plans and the amount that can be set aside by such plans on a tax-exempt basis. Also requires management to explain to employees the technical concepts introduced by the **Employee Retirement Income Security Act of 1974** and its amendments, particularly matters relating to pension plans. *See also* Omnibus Budget Reconciliation Act of 1990; Tax Reform Act of 1986.

Deficit-reduction Reconciliation Act of 1989 Established a fee scale for physicians' services under Medicare and limited the amount that physicians could bill patients above what Medicare pays. Medicare generally pays 80 percent of the allowable fee for a particular service, and the patient pays the remaining 20 percent. Physicians who do not accept Medicare's rate as full payment are prohibited by law from charging more than 120 percent (in 1992) and 114 percent (in 1993) of that rate.

defined benefit Keogh plan A plan for self-employed individuals operating in unincorporated businesses. Similar to **defined benefit pension plans**.

defined benefit pension plan A plan that entitles participants to retirement benefits established in advance. Each year the amount of annual contributions required to provide the defined benefit is determined based on actuarial assumptions such as pre- and postretirement interest, mortality, turnover, salary scale, and so on. Although retirement benefits are fixed, contributions vary from year to year. The annual benefit at retirement is limited to 100 percent of gross income up to $94,023 (adjusted annually for cost of living). The benefit can be increased or decreased depending on whether retirement benefits begin before or after the individual's Social Security retirement age. *See also* cash balance pension plan.

defined benefit plan (DBP) A plan that uses a formula that includes earnings and length of service to calculate the retirement benefits of employees. The employer promises a certain level of benefits at retirement regardless of what happens. The level of entitlement is predefined in terms of any one or a combination of factors, such as level of pay, years of service, and age. The DBP is the type of plan used by most major companies nationwide. For example, a corporate pension plan is a defined benefit. *See also* guaranteed investment contract.

defined contribution plan (DCP) A retirement plan in which the benefit is not set in advance but depends on plan earnings, length of service, and the amount of annual contributions. DCPs offer flexibility and control for both the employer and the employee. Retirement benefits are determined by the contributions made by the employee and the employer and their earnings during the period between the contributions and the date of retirement. Benefits are not guaranteed. The employer merely promises to put in a certain amount of money (determined by such things as profit, percentage of salary, or an employment-related formula), which the employee may augment in most plans. Contributions are invested on behalf of the named employee, and retirement benefits are whatever accumulated contributions and their investment yield add up to when the employee ceases work. These plans have the advantage of being portable. *See also* age-based defined contribution plan; deferred profit-sharing plan; Section 401(k), Internal Revenue Code; thrift savings plan.

delayed retirement credit Under the Social Security system, people who continue to work and do not receive some or all of their monthly checks because of the earnings test are given what is called delayed retirement credit. In effect, it is a bonus for continuing to work beyond age 65. The credit is worth 3.5 percent a year for those who became 65 in 1990 and 1991, rising to 8 percent for those becoming age 62 in 2005 or later.

delivery system Means of conducting training or learning, from on-the-job training, job or work aids, exportable training packages, and correspondence courses, to classroom training, multimedia, interactive video, computer-based training, and self-study.

demand forecast A forecast developed from analysis of the projected work load over a specified time frame, usually five years. It may take two forms: a core forecast, which consists of the most certain definition of personnel needs, and a variable forecast, which incorporates less certain variables and permits the inclusion of "what if" scenarios. Actual planning is invariably based on the core forecast, and the variable forecast is held in reserve. *See also* availability forecast.

dental capitation plan (DCP) A plan that pays dentists a small monthly fee per patient whether service is provided or not.

dental care plan (DCP) Similar to medical and hospitalization plans, a DCP includes provisions relating to eligibility, cost-sharing, and determination of benefits. Full reimbursements are limited to minor preventive and restorative procedures. Major restorative (crowns and dentures) and orthodontic (cosmetic) procedures are rarely covered for more than 50 to 75 percent of the cost.

dental preferred provider organization (DPPO) A dental plan in which an employer contracts with a dentist or group of dentists to provide dental care for its employees. Dentists in the network are paid on a traditional fee-for-service basis but at lower rates, typically giving employees a 10 to 30 percent discount. Although designed to improve monitoring of plan utilization and effect savings, they may not achieve the latter due to increased utilization caused by participating dentists offsetting corporate-negotiated discounts by increasing the number of treatments or office visits.

dependent care assistance plan (DCAP) Under the Economic Recovery Tax Act of 1981, employers were given the opportunity to offer dependent care assistance in the form of payments or help in finding adequate child care facilities as a fringe benefit to their employees. *See also* voucher program.

dependent care program (DCP) Includes **child care** and **elder care.** There are four categories of options: financial assistance programs, establishment of child care facilities, workplace information services, and personnel policies.

dependent care reimbursement (DCR) A relatively new employee benefit in which the employer reimburses employees for dependent care expenditures either fully or in part.

dependent coverage waiver (DCW) A health care cost reduction strategy. Employees are allowed to waive dependent coverage.

deposit administration arrangement (DAA) A relatively new funding plan vehicle for annuity contracts. Instead of purchasing or insuring pensions for active employees, the assets of these plans are maintained in an accumulation account (an unallocated fund accruing interest). When an employee retires, his or her pension (the amount of which is then known) is purchased from the insurance annuity account and the purchase price is subtracted from the accumulation account. Key features of the plan are: (1) greater flexibility than under conventional plans; (2) less extensive guarantees than under fully insured plans such as deferred group annuities or retirement income contracts; (3) purchased benefits for retirees calculated according to the carrier's dividend formula and the experience of all purchased annuities rather than according to the experience of individual deposit administration contracts; and (4) the contract is allocated for retired participants and unallocated for actives. *See also* guaranteed investment contract.

de-skilling The practice of dividing low-end manufacturing and service jobs into the smallest and simplest tasks in an attempt to increase efficiency, measurability, and consistency in performance. The reverse of up-skilling.

destination services Services established to help relocating or transferring employees to adapt to their new surroundings, such as home marketing assistance, school, child day care, and elder care information, and spousal reemployment assistance.

detoxification facility In health benefits, an institution licensed or certified by the state to provide alcoholism or drug dependency treatment and where such treatment is supervised by a physician or qualified staff member of the treatment facility.

deunionization The termination of union representation for a particular collective bargaining unit. It is accomplished by a decertification election in which workers vote to disband their union. Also called *deauthorization* or *decertification*.

development A planned set of learning experiences designed to improve the skills and job performance of individuals in their current positions in a defined career field or a specific job or to prepare them for advancement to higher-level, more responsible positions in the organization. *See also* career development.

developmental counseling A form of supervisory counseling in which the employee and the supervisor share ideas and the process of identifying alternatives and selecting the means of remedying a deficiency or solving a problem. *See also* career counseling; job performance counseling; personal adjustment counseling.

diagnosis-related groups (DRGs) Medicare reimbursement levels passed by the Congress in 1983 to control the costs of government health care programs. If a hospital's charges for a particular diagnosis exceed the standard established by the DRGs, reimbursement is reduced to the amount allowed and the provider must absorb the difference. *See also* resource-based relative value scale.

diagnostic survey A survey designed and conducted to analyze a specific organizational or employee problem or situation identified by some other means. The survey is conducted to uncover the reasons for it, probe feelings about the situation or problem, and get ideas for its solution.

diagnostic test A test used to identify, locate, assess, and analyze an individual's specific areas of strength and weakness, and where possible, determine their cause. Commonly used to identify knowledge and skills deficiencies. *See also* performance test.

didactic learning/teaching Traditional instructor-centered, pedagogic, or instructor-directed learning. It makes use of the presentation and question-and-answer (Socratic) approaches. *See also* andragogy.

directive appraisal One-way or one-sided evaluation. The superior observes, evaluates, and provides feedback on performance to subordinates, who are allowed little or no input to the process. The manager establishes the standards, chooses the measures, does the evaluating, reports findings to subordinates at an appraisal interview, makes suggestions for improvement, and records the results.

directive counseling A process in which counselors serve as coaches and teachers. They collect, sift, organize, classify, summarize, and evaluate relevant information to arrive at a description of the circumstances surrounding the client's problem. They analyze attitudes, motives, interests, emotional balance, and other factors that may facilitate or inhibit satisfactory adjustment or solution to the client's problem. Counselors may advise, persuade, or explain. *See also* nondirective counseling.

direct reimbursement dental A means of saving time and money and increasing the flexibility of employee dental benefits plans. Employees are reimbursed directly for certain dental and orthodontic procedures within a matter of days on a fixed scale; for example, 100 percent of the first $100, 80 percent of the next $500 up to an annual maximum reimbursement of $750 per covered person.

disability 1. As defined by the Rehabilitation Act of 1973 and the **Americans with Disabilities Act of 1990**: (1) a physical or mental impairment that substantially limits one or more of the major life activities of an individual; (2) a record of such an impairment; or (3) being regarded as having such an impairment. It does not include such conditions as transvestism, transsexualism, voyeurism, gender identity disorders not resulting from physical impairments, other sexual behavior disorders, compulsive gambling, kleptomania, pyromania, and psychoactive substance use disorders resulting from current illegal use of drugs. **2.** Under Social Security, a person is considered disabled only if he or she is unable to do any kind of work for which suited, and only if inability to work is expected to last for at least a year or to result in death. Therefore, it does not include partial disabilities or short-term disabilities. Benefits continue as long as the individual remains disabled. **3.** In general, disability includes persons who are physically disabled, mentally impaired, emotionally impaired, learning disabled, and people who must use wheelchairs, crutches, canes, or walkers. *See also* disability benefits; occupational disability.

disability benefits Benefits paid to a disabled employee. A disabled employee is usually defined as one who has a physical or mental condition(s) that prevents the worker from engaging in any substantial gainful work, and the condition is expected to last for a specified period (typically 12 or more months) or result in death. Medical proof is invariably required to support an application for disability benefits. Includes Department of Veterans Affairs disability benefits; state and local government disability benefits; private insurance disability benefits; Supplemental Security Income benefits; Social Security disability benefits; Workers' Compensation. *See also* disability.

disability case management (DCM) Case-by-case monitoring of the treatment of employees with disabilities. *See also* disability management.

Disability Determination Service (DDS) A state agency that makes decisions for the Social Security Administration as to whether an individual claimant qualifies for disability benefits. DDS evaluation teams, composed of a disability examiner and a physician or psychologist, make the determination using very specific medical and vocational criteria, although many such determinations are made solely on the basis of a treating physician's evidence and recommendations.

disability management Assigning a single individual responsibility for coordinating and managing disability benefits within an organization. Designed to retain and rehabilitate employees with disabilities and put into place innovative disability management services. *See also* disability case management.

disciplinary layoff A form of disciplinary action involving suspension, usually without pay for a specified number of days or weeks, but almost never for longer than one month.

discipline Traditionally, discipline has meant complete and total obedience to rules and regulations and to the orders and directives of superiors. Failure to comply resulted in punitive actions. Today, discipline is seen as involving self-control and a sense of personal responsibility for conduct, behavior, and performance. A disciplined organization is one in which members willingly adhere to the rules and principles governing conduct as set forth by the appropriate authorities. Because they accept the rules as right, they are willing to subordinate themselves to the organization.

disclosure agreement A document that clearly describes the responsibility of the employee to protect company secrets or other items of value to the organization, defines what items are included in that category, and identifies the penalties for violation. It is signed by new employees, witnessed by a corporate official, and filed. *See also* confidentiality agreement.

discrimination Any policy, procedure, or action that tends to place an individual or group at an unfair disadvantage in the recruitment, screening, selection, assignment, compensation, testing, training, development, or promotion processes. To prove discrimination, an employee must establish that he or she belongs to a protected class, was rejected although qualified for the job, and that the employer filled the position with an individual not in the protected class. To rebut a claim of discrimination, employers must refute employees' claims or establish a defense based on one of the following: discharge for gross misconduct, poor performance, or reduction in force. *See also* affirmative action; Age Discrimination in Employment Act of 1967; Americans with Disabilities Act of 1990; equal employment opportunity; Equal Pay Act of 1963; Pregnancy Discrimination Act of 1978; Title VII.

disparate impact A legal term relating to a form of discrimination in which an employment practice or procedure (such as a psychological test) results in discrimination against a protected class. Such a practice is unlawful unless the employer can demonstrate that the practice is either job-related or a business necessity. Federal agencies have adopted the following formula to determine when disparate impact exists: a selection rate for any racial, ethnic, or gender group that is less than 80 percent of the rate for the highest selection rate. Also referred to as *disparate treatment* and *disparate rejection rates*. *See also* discrimination; population comparison; Title VII.

displacement Describes workers who have lost their jobs as a result of economic change, such as plant closings and layoffs due to shifts in consumer preferences, foreign competition, automation, and robotics. *See also* employment displacement; job displacement.

disposable worker *See* contingent work force; sheddable worker.

distance training or education In general, education and training provided for adults at remote locations by such means as satellite-delivered training and interactive video. John R. Verduin, Jr., and Thomas A. Clark (*Distance Education: The Foundations of Effective Practice*) define distance training or education as "any formal approach to learning in which a majority of the instruction occurs while educator and learner are at a distance from one another."

diversity program A program designed to help employees at all levels of the organization learn new attitudes and adopt new behaviors relating to cultural differences. Includes encouraging diversity in the work force as a priority through hiring practices, creating new internal personnel structures and systems to monitor performance, holding managers accountable for promoting a multicultural work environment, and establishing diversity training and development programs.

diversity training A generic term used to describe any type of training designed to help people understand and value cultural differences in the workplace. Usually provided for managers and supervisors.

dividend equivalent plan A form of stock equivalent plan in which a number of units of **phantom stock** is granted to an executive, each of which creates rights to a payment equal to any dividends paid on a share of the company's stock.

dock 1. A penalty for worker tardiness in which the employee loses pay for the lost time. **2.** Sometimes used to describe other penalties for tardiness such as the requirement to make up lost time or be subjected to disciplinary action.

docking rules Federal rules governing the reduction of employee pay for time off the job for reasons other than sickness or accident; for example, tardiness or leaving the job before quitting time. Under the law, salaried workers cannot collect overtime pay nor have their pay docked for taking a few hours off to do such things as take care of personal business. Under the Fair Labor Standards Act of 1938, a salaried employee who is treated like an an hourly worker is eligible for overtime pay and can seek back overtime pay for up to two years. However, under the docking rules, an employer can reduce the pay of a salaried worker if he or she is absent for an entire week, away from the job for an entire day for reasons other than sickness or accident, or is absent for more than a day for reasons of sickness or disability when the employee is covered by a paid-leave policy.

domestic partner Used by organizations, including insurance carriers, to describe a person who lives with an employee or the insured in a relationship, whether gay or straight. *See also* significant other.

double coverage Describes the situation where spouses with access to and eligibility for work-related health insurance coverage both enroll in the program.

double dipping/dipper 1. Collecting two (or even three) pensions; for example, military retirement, Social Security, and federal, state, or municipal annuities. **2.** Accepting federal full-time employment following retirement from military service with an annuity. **3.** The practice of counting a spouse's monthly benefits as income for the purpose of determining alimony payments when a lump-sum settlement has been previously granted (disallowed by the courts).

downgrading 1. Moving a job or position to a lower level in a general schedule or job evaluation system. **2.** Moving an individual job incumbent to a lower-level job or pay grade.

downshifting Describes a career move that involves trading off higher pay and the power of a prestigious job for one that provides a lower salary and status to fulfill personal and family needs and priorities. For example, a fast-track middle manager or executive in a large corporation who decides to resign and accept a small-town secondary school teaching position.

downwardly mobile professional (DOMO) Typically applied to a person under age 40 who has given up a high-paying job to pursue a more satisfying way of life.

drill and practice A learning strategy that involves practice under supervision of some of the steps in a specific process with critique and feedback. For example, a drill in a golf lesson might focus on hitting balls embedded in a fairway bunker (rather than balls lying cleanly on top of the sand in a bunker near the green).

drug formulary In prescription drugs benefits plans, a specific list of drugs by therapeutic grouping that must be prescribed before benefits are received (or are preferred). Formularies are designed by the pharmacy network provider and a multidisciplinary committee of physicians and pharmacists [Pharmacy and Therapeutics (P&T) Committee]. Each therapeutic group is studied, and drugs are ranked according to clinical effectiveness and cost. The network provider then issues a request for proposals to drug manufacturers. Upon receipt of the proposals, the provider and the P&T committee designate the drugs within each therapeutic group that will be included in the formulary. *See also* therapeutic drug utilization review.

Drug-Free Workplace Act of 1988 (DFWA) Legislation that took effect March 18, 1989. Requires organizations receiving federal contracts of $25,000 or more to meet requirements designed to keep their workplaces free of illegal drugs. It also applies to any organization receiving a grant (including universities) no matter what the amount. To comply, companies must publish and distribute a policy prohibiting the unlawful manufacture, distribution, dispensing, possession, or use of controlled substances in the workplace; notify federal authorities of any convictions of employees for illegal drug activity in the workplace; provide for penalties for employees convicted of drug-related violations on the job; establish an employee-awareness program on the dangers and penalties of workplace drug abuse; and notify employees of the availability of resources for drug rehabilitation and counseling. Violators are penalized by loss of all federal business or grants and face possible disbarment from future opportunities for up to five years.

drug program A health care cost-reduction strategy in which arrangements are made with local pharmacies to waive employee charges if a generic drug is used (these charges are paid by the sponsoring company), and the difference between the generic and name brand is charged to the employee if the latter is chosen.

drug testing 1. Testing employees for use of narcotics and alcohol. **2.** Regulations issued by the Department of Health and Human Services in 1988 require employers of certain types of workers to conduct five kinds of drug testing for the presence of marijuana, cocaine, opiates, amphetamines, and PCP: random, preemployment, periodic, reasonable-cause, and postaccident. Workers include those involved in airline-related functions, railroad operations, interstate truck and bus driving, mass transit, the merchant marines, and natural gas and hazardous liquid pipeline operations. **3.** Rules for drug testing of interstate truck and bus drivers, aviation industry employees, mass transit workers, railroad workers, mariners on commercial vessels, and pipeline industry employees promulgated by the Department of Transportation in November 1989. They require preemployment, periodic, reasonable-cause, postaccident, and random testing for marijuana, cocaine, opiates, amphetamines, and phencyclidine (PCP). *See also* Transportation Act of 1989.

drug utilization review (DUR) A program for screening prescription drug transactions for potential overdosing or dangerous drug interventions. Administered by in-house or contracted utilization review officers, companies, or committees. *See also* therapeutic drug utilization review.

dual career tracks An approach to employee career development that involves permitting people to move back and forth between managerial and technical or professional jobs over the course of their careers and at the same time allowing them to move up in status and compensation. The strategy is adopted to improve retention, motivation, job satisfaction, and performance as well as result in the production of creative ideas, practices, and products. Also called *dual career ladders*.

dual motive case A provision of the Civil Rights Act of 1991 in which an employer, while making an employment decision, relies on both permissible and impermissible factors. Where formerly the employer could prevail by proving that the decision would have been the same even if the unlawful factor were absent, the Act makes the burden of proof more difficult. The employee charging discrimination will prevail if it is proven that his or her protected status (race, sex, and so on) was a "motivating factor" in the decision regardless of other factors. In essence, the employer must demonstrate that only lawful factors were used to make the decision.

dues check-off An arrangement negotiated by a union whereby the employer deducts dues from the worker's pay and turns the money over to the union.

durable medical equipment Equipment that serves a medical purpose, cannot be useful to people who are not sick or injured, can be used repeatedly, and is prescribed by a physician for use in the home. It typically includes such items as oxygen equipment and wheelchairs and may include seat lift chairs, power-operated vehicles, equipment for care of pressure sores, and transcutaneous electrical nerve stimulators.

durable power of attorney for health care A legal (in some states) means of appointing another person to make health care decisions for incapacitated individuals. Because general powers of attorney become null and void when the maker becomes incompetent, some states now permit a power of attorney to be designated as "durable" when stated in the document. An alternative to a living will and often used in conjunction with one.

duty One of the major subdivisions of the work (job) performed by one individual. A duty has these characteristics: It is one of the incumbent's major functions; it occupies all or a reasonable portion of the incumbent's time; it consists of a cluster of closely related tasks; it occurs with reasonable frequency during the work cycle; it involves work operations that use closely related skills, knowledge, and abilities; and it is performed for some purpose, by some method, according to some standard with respect to speed, accuracy, quality, or quantity. For example, the duties of an electronics equipment repairer include inspecting, adjusting, aligning, troubleshooting, servicing, and repairing. *See also* element; job; task.

E

EAP	Employee assistance program.
ECF	Extended care facility.
EDWAAA	Economic Dislocation and Worker Adjustment Assistance Act of 1988.
EEAA	Employee Educational Assistance Act of 1978.
EEO	Equal employment opportunity.
EEOA	Equal Employment Opportunity Act of 1972.
EEOC	Equal Employment Opportunity Commission.
EHOP	Employee home ownership plan.
EI	Employee involvement.
EPA	Equal Pay Act of 1963.
EPPA	Employee Polygraph Protection Act of 1988.
ERIP	Early retirement incentive program.
ERISA	Employee Retirement Income Security Act of 1974.
ERTA	Economic Recovery Tax Act of 1981.
ESOP	Employee stock option (ownership) plan.
ET	Embedded training.
89	*See* Section 89, Internal Revenue Code.

early retirement incentive program (ERIP) A strategy designed to encourage retirement of older employees or when budgetary pressures require a significant reduction in personnel within a relatively short period of time. ERIPs have been adopted by many organizations since the passage of the Age Discrimination in Employment Act (as amended in 1987), which prohibits mandatory retirement for most jobs at any age. They have also been used when economic conditions require downsizing or restructuring. Essentially, such plans establish a period (open window) of from 30 to 90 days during which eligible employees may voluntarily retire with a one-time monetary incentive as well as a full pension—and sometimes additional fringe benefits. Eligibility may be based on age (anyone over age 65), years of continuous service, or both (for example, the **Rule of 75.**

earned entitlements Work-related benefits, such as annuities and health insurance, which were paid for in part by deductions from income during the work life of the beneficiary. *See also* entitlements; granted entitlements.

economic benefit A term used by the Internal Revenue Service to identify and determine current tax liability when the employee can receive compensation (backed by a funded plan and instrument, rights that are nonforfeitable, and with no risk of forfeiture) even though he or she may elect not to do so.

Economic Dislocation and Worker Adjustment Assistance Act of 1988 (EDWAAA) Amends Title III of the **Job Training Partnership Act of 1982** dealing with dislocated workers: terminated, long-term unemployed, and self-employed underemployed blue-collar workers, white-collar workers, mid-level managers, other self-employed people, and displaced homemakers without any economic criteria for assistance. Beginning July 1989, the program was operated at both state and local levels and required states to allocate funds to provide services locally to dislocated workers, such as classroom training, occupational skills development, and on-the-job training. It also permitted states to provide out-of-area job search and relocation assistance, basic and remedial education, training in English as a second language, entrepreneurial training, and other job-related training. In addition, the Act provides readjustment services, including testing and assessment and developing individual readjustment plans.

Economic Recovery Tax Act of 1981 (ERTA) Authorized the establishment of incentive stock option plans and granted deferral of tax liability until the stock is sold. The Act also permitted the establishment of individual retirement accounts for anyone who earned an income regardless of whether the individual was already enrolled in a company pension plan. That provision has since been extensively modified. Another of its provisions gave employers the opportunity to offer dependent care assistance plans to employees as a fringe benefit.

education Learning programs that are not job-oriented. They are designed to enrich a person's general knowledge and capabilities over the long term, not to prepare him or her for a profession or an occupation. *See also* human resources development; training.

edutainment Describes a combination of educational and entertaining programming used in corporate video. Edutainment employs such familiar network formats as magazine shows, newscasts, and game shows to inform, educate, train, and entertain.

elder care Services provided to the elderly (grandparents, parents, and spouses), including information and consultation, seminars and workshops, on-site peer support groups, and facilities for day care. *See also* child care.

Electromation decision A December 1992 decision of the National Labor Relations Board on the legality of employee action committees or similar team-based work groups. The board ruled that employee committees formed at Electromation, Inc., an Indiana electronics firm, were "labor organizations" that violated federal labor laws because of the employer's alleged interference with and domination over the committees. In August 1993, the NLRB ruled that a committee is a labor organization if the organization exists to deal with employees on mandatory bargaining subjects (e.g., grievances, pay, hours, working conditions). Unresolved is whether any such program that exists to achieve quality or efficiency constitutes a labor organization. *See also* Gissel bargaining order.

Electronic Communications Privacy Act of 1986 Prohibits interception of electronic mail by any extra-organizational third party, including government and law enforcement agencies and individuals, without proper authority, such as a search warrant. Although designed to ensure privacy, absolute security of interoffice, computerized systems is unattainable (unless encrypted by sophisticated codes). They invariably leave an electronic trail, which can be used to recover the messages. Although it is illegal in some states for an employer to listen in on private conversations and telephone calls, there are no clear-cut rules covering electronic mail. In some cases the courts have ruled that, because the company owned the computer system, it had the right to read anything created on it.

electronic performance support system An integrated computerized system, composed of a database and support functions that provide on-line assistance to workers in the form of advice, assistance, data, tools, and images as the main features of intelligent workstations.

element The smallest unit of work activity described in occupational or job analysis. Elements are the smallest steps into which it is practicable to subdivide any work operation or task without analyzing separate motions, movements, and mental processes. They are also the work units that deal with the details of how the methods, procedures, and techniques involved in a task are carried out. They are very important to developers of training systems. For example, elements performed by an electronics repairer include soldering and unsoldering connections, activating switches, and tightening screws. *See also* duty; job; task.

eligible small business In relation to the Internal Revenue Code and the **Americans with Disabilities Act of 1990,** a business whose gross receipts do not exceed $1 million or whose work force does not consist of more than 30 full-time workers. Such businesses may qualify for a deduction of up to $15,000 per year for expenses associated with the removal of qualified architectural and transportation barriers and a tax credit of up to 50 percent of eligible access expenditures that exceed $250 but do not exceed $10,250.

elimination period The number of consecutive days an individual must be confined in a nursing home or alternate long-term care facility to qualify for benefits under a long-term care insurance policy. The elimination period initiates a covered period of confinement.

embedded training (ET) Training that is built into the software of computer applications programs—the programs the employee uses on the job—rather than provided in a separate training package. ET is on the same terminal or delivery device as the product it supports. An example is a program that teaches an employee how to use a spreadsheet while using the spreadsheet itself. *See also* competency-based training.

emergency child care services (ECCS) A form of direct employer-supported child care service that involves making emergency arrangements, especially when a child is ill, such as helping pay for special sick-child infirmaries or family day care homes, or providing health care workers to go to the child's home. Some companies extend the service to situations where usual parental child care arrangements are upset. In such cases, a trained caregiver is sent to the employee's home. *See also* on-site or near-site child care center.

employee 1. In general, an individual who works for wages or a salary for a company or an individual. **2.** As defined by the Internal Revenue Service, an employee is a person who works for wages or a salary and whose labor and how it is performed are controlled by the employer. *See also* independent contractor.

employee assistance program (EAP) A program designed to help organizations identify and diagnose a variety of problems and counsel and assist employees in dealing with those problems and issues, such as drug and alcohol abuse, child and spouse abuse, emotional problems, family and social problems, financial problems, career problems, legal concerns, stress management, vocational rehabilitation, and mental and emotional illness.

Employee Educational Assistance Act of 1978 (EEAA) Codified as Section 127 of the Internal Revenue Code, the EEAA exempted employees from paying taxes on employer-provided tuition reimbursement benefits for non-job-related college course work (but not courses related to sports or hobbies) through the 1983 tax year. Following expiration of the law December 31, 1983, Public Law 98-611 was passed in 1984 retroactively extending EEAA to cover the 1984 and 1985 tax years. For the first time, the law imposed an annual limit of $5,000 as the maximum amount of reimbursement that employees could exclude from their taxable income. When the law expired December 31, 1985, the Tax Reform Act of 1986 (Public Law 99-514) was passed. It granted another retroactive two-year extension of EEAA. In November 1988, the Technical Corrections and Miscellaneous Revenue Act extended EEAA for 51 days to cover the 1988 tax year retroactively. The Act limits the exemption to undergraduate courses taken to maintain or improve skills employees need in their current jobs or to provide new skills that employers or the law requires employees to develop to keep their present jobs. In addition, the bill limited EEAA exclusions to reimbursements received for undergraduate courses only (earlier bills applied to graduate courses as well). In November 1989, the Congress voted to extend the benefit through September 30, 1990, through the Omnibus Budget Reconciliation Act of 1989. The Act limited EEAA exclusions to $5,250 or less, and tuition reimbursements for graduate studies were ineligible. The Revenue Act of 1992 extended the tax exclusion for employer-provided educational assistance. Retroactive reinstatement and permanent extension bill pending in Congress in 1993.

employee home ownership plan (EHOP) A benefits plan designed to assist employees to finance the purchase of a home. Employers help their employees find affordable housing and help them finance it. For example, shares of stock contributed by an employer could be used as collateral for borrowing money loaned to employees toward a down payment. The plan would also allow first-time home buyers to use tax-sheltered retirement savings vehicles, such as IRAs and 401(k) plans, toward a down payment on a home. Requires congressional approval. *See also* equity sharing.

employee involvement (EI) The process of engaging workers as individuals and in groups at all levels of organization in making decisions relating to their work. It is characterized by three elements: information, empowerment, and rewards. *See also* Electromation decision; Gissel bargaining order.

Employee Polygraph Protection Act of 1988 (EPPA) An Act preventing most private employers from requesting or requiring any employee or prospective employee to submit to any lie detector test, requesting or using the results of such tests, or discharging, disciplining, or otherwise discriminating against any employee or prospective employee on the basis of the results of such tests. Exempt from the Act are federal government agencies engaged in intelligence or counterintelligence functions (FBI, National Security Agency, Defense Intelligence Agency, and CIA), organizations that manufacture and distribute controlled substances, and those involved in the protection of nuclear power plants, public transportation, currency, commodities, or proprietary information. Polygraphs may still be administered under severely restricted conditions as a part of an investigation involving suspected wrongdoing. However, employees may refuse to undergo a polygraph test, and they may not be discharged, disciplined, or denied promotions solely on polygraph results.

employee prefunding A health benefit cost-reduction strategy for post-retirement health care benefits. The plan requires active employees to contribute to their retiree health plan by making monthly premium payments based on age. Contributions are returned with interest if the employee leaves the company before retirement. *See also* fixed-dollar benefits; graduated benefits.

Employee Retirement Income Security Act of 1974 (ERISA) An act that regulates employee benefits such as health care, sickness and accident, disability, and death benefits as well as retirement and capital accumulation plans. It created government-run employer-financed corporations to protect employees against pension fund failures. The Act covers eligibility, funding arrangements, fiduciary responsibilities, and other standards, including financing, vesting, and administration of pension plans in most private businesses and industries. It requires employers to maintain records on employee health and welfare plans and pension plans and descriptions of those plans and report to the Department of Labor, IRS, and Pension Benefits Guarantee Corporation. ERISA has been modified by virtually every comprehensive budget and tax law since its enactment.

employee rights In the context of labor-management relations, employees are protected against unfair labor practices, enterprise interference with employee rights, discrimination in conditions of employment that tend to discourage or encourage membership in a union, and discrimination against an employee for filing a grievance or giving testimony. *See also* Fair Labor Standards Act of 1938; Weingarten Rule (or Rights).

employee stock option (ownership) plan (ESOP) Under such a plan, the benefits of a capital owner are given to employees as an incentive. After they have become vested in the program, employees can redeem their stock when they leave the company through resignation, termination, or retirement. Companies sell bonds, borrow funds from banks, savings and loan institutions, mutual funds, insurance companies, and large institutional investors, or set aside stock. In 1989, Congress repealed the interest exclusion on loans to employee stock ownership plans unless at least 30 percent of company stock is in the hands of employees. *See also* payroll-based stock option plan; performance award plan.

employer coalition Originally, an informal arrangement whereby management, labor, insurers, and health care providers collected and shared data on health care utilization. Employer coalitions have now been transformed into coalition purchasing groups called health care purchasing organizations.

employment-at-will A legal doctrine maintaining that it is the right of an employer or employee to terminate the employment relationship at any time and for any—or no—reason. The doctrine has been successfully challenged by employees in the courts in recent years. *See also* wrongful discharge.

employment displacement Involuntary termination of a worker because the job has been eliminated. *See also* displacement; job displacement.

employment practices liability insurance A policy that covers the costs of litigating employee claims, such as discrimination, sexual harassment, wrongful discharge, failure to promote, breach of employment contract, misrepresentation, and defamation. Typically does not cover losses from violations of **Employee Retirement Income Security Act** (ERISA), **Occupational Safety and Health Act** (OSHA), **Consolidated Omnibus Budget Reconciliation Act** (COBRA), and labor relations, securities, and workers' compensation laws.

employment tests Tests used in the employee selection process. Section 106 of the **Civil Rights Act of 1991,** which became effective November 26, 1991, states, "It shall be an unlawful employment practice for a respondent, in connection with the selection or referral of applicants or candidates for employment or promotion, to adjust the scores of, use different cutoff scores for, or otherwise alter the results of, employment related tests on the basis of race, color, religion, sex, or national origin." In effect, the Act placed the burden of proof on employers to show that there is a business necessity for their tests.

employment torts Grounds for employee lawsuits, the most common of which are invasion of privacy, deceit, intentional interference with contractual relations, and wrongful discharge.

empowered profit sharing A means of enhancing growth in employee morale and productivity and corporate profitability. Involves combining or blending employee **empowerment** and profit or **gain sharing** bonus systems. It uses profit sharing plans, regular and frequent communication on financial results, corporative initiatives, and the solicitation of worker opinions on how the organization can improve its operations to encourage workers to view themselves as partners in the business venture.

empowerment Helping people to take charge of their work life. Giving employees responsibility, ownership of their jobs, power over what and how things are done, decision-making authority, and recognition for their ideas and knowledge to improve their performance and productivity. Turning employees loose with the proper training and motivation and encouraging them to get out there and do whatever needs to be done.

entitlements 1. Benefits that are totally associated with private or public employment, such as vacations, holidays, overtime, educational assistance, and matching gifts. **2.** Government (federal, state, or municipal) benefits such as Social Security, Medicare, Medicaid, unemployment compensation, and so on. *See also* earned entitlements; equity benefits; granted entitlements; protection benefits; statutory benefits.

entry-level training Training provided to new employees to ensure that they get a good start. It is usually provided for operative employees. It is invariably scheduled for technicians and supervisory personnel upon their initial employment in an HR-related position.

environmental training A form of technical training, usually conducted by subject matter experts such as chemists and engineers, that focuses on federal and state laws and regulations governing air emissions, water polluting substances, and solid waste disposal. The training is designed to keep employees in compliance with laws and regulations and communities safe from toxic waste and hazardous emissions and conditions. Regulating agencies include the Environmental Protection Agency, Office of Safety and Health Administration, and Department of Transportation.

equal employment opportunity (EEO) A policy guaranteeing equal opportunity to all prospective and current employees and stating that no employee or applicant will be discriminated against because of race, color, age, sex, national origin, religion, or handicap; that affirmative action will be taken to ensure that equal opportunity is provided to all employees; and that positive actions will be taken to recruit, employ, and promote qualified persons underrepresented or underemployed in the work force, with particular attention to African-Americans, Hispanics, Asians and Pacific Islanders, American Indians, Alaskan natives, women, and persons with disabilities. These provisions also apply to screening and selection, assignment and transfer, promotion, compensation and benefits, training and development, discipline, and layoffs and termination. *See also* Americans with Disabilities Act of 1990; Civil Rights Act of 1964; discrimination; Equal Employment Opportunity Act of 1972; protected class.

Equal Employment Opportunity Act of 1972 (EEOA) An amendment to **Title VII** of the **Civil Rights Act of 1964** that made it unlawful to discriminate on the basis of race, color, religion, sex, or national origin in hiring and discharge and in limiting, segregating, or classifying employees or applicants. Administered by the Equal Employment Opportunity Commission. *See also* Civil Rights Act of 1964; equal employment opportunity.

Equal Pay Act of 1963 (EPA) An amendment to the **Fair Labor Standards Act of 1938** that prohibits sex-based pay differences where the work performed is equal in terms of skills, effort, and responsibility (doctrine of equal pay for equal work). Exceptions include bona fide seniority, merit- or production-based pay systems, or any other job-related factor other than gender. It is applicable to private industry as well as to federal, state, and local governments. To ensure compliance, employers need data to analyze pay and job content by sex. Administered by the Fair Labor Standards Board. *See also* Bennet Amendment; comparable worth; discrimination.

equal treatment A legal doctrine pertaining to cases of unlawful discharge. It asks, "Has the employer applied its rules and penalties to all employees evenhandedly and without discrimination?"

equity adjustment A permanent salary increase added to an employee's salary because analysis has demonstrated that the person's salary, salary range, or grade increase was too low relative to comparable positions. Merit or cost of living is not a factor.

equity benefits Benefits that increase in value in connection with one or more of the following: years of service, rate of pay, and age. Examples are pension plans, profit-sharing plans, thrift savings plans, cash-deferred (401[k]) plans, individual retirement accounts, and stock options. *See also* benefits; deferred benefits plan; deferred compensation; entitlements.

equity sharing (ES) A form of employer-assisted housing benefits. Formerly used almost exclusively as loans to get employees to accept assignments in high-cost areas, ES is now more broadly employed. For example, some companies gradually convey full ownership of property to an employee without also transferring potential financial problems by granting employees an annual equity transfer each year that the employee remains with the company. In addition to spreading loans over a longer period of time, insurance policies may also be taken out to help the employee's dependents gain full ownership of the property should the employee die or become disabled. *See also* employee home ownership plan.

ERISA bond A fidelity bond required by federal law that insures tax-qualified pension plans against theft and embezzlement. Must be obtained by all plan trustees and others who handle plan funds. *See also* Form 5500 filings; summary annual report; summary plan description.

escalator clause A provision in a collective bargaining agreement for making upward or downward wage adjustments in accordance with changes in the cost of living.

executive transformation Learner-centered programs designed to convert *functional* managers and specialists into *general* managers—people who can manage across several organizational functions and make strategic decisions that overcome the inherently insular and conflicting goals of those functions.

exempt employee An employee exempt from minimum wage and overtime provisions of the **Fair Labor Standards Act of 1938.** Exempt employees include bona fide executives, managers, supervisors, professionals, administrators, and sales personnel who are salaried or commissioned.

expedited arbitration A form of alternative dispute resolution used by the American Arbitration Association to resolve cases involving small claims under several sets of rules. Hearings are scheduled by phone and are concluded in a day or less. *See also* alternative dispute resolution procedure; fact-finding; med-arb.

exploding A form of fraud or dishonesty (chicanery) practiced by unscrupulous physicians and other health care practitioners to increase their income. Exemplified by the submission of a bill to the insurer for a series of tests that have all been done on a single sample of blood, thereby tripling or quadrupling the dollar value of the claim.

extended care facility (ECF) A health care facility that provides medical care for individuals requiring extended care, including patients who have been discharged from a hospital.

external evaluation In training and development, assessment of the results within or outside of the organization when employees are assigned to or return to the job. Evaluation may focus on changes in job behavior and performance of employees or organization changes attributable to the program or programs offered. *See also* immediate evaluation; ultimate evaluation.

F

FAP   Financial assistance program.
FBP   Flexible benefits/flex benefits program.
FCP   Family care program.
FCRA   Fair Credit Reporting Act of 1969.
FICA   Federal Insurance Contributions Act of 1935.
FLSA   Fair Labor Standards Act of 1938.
FMLA   Family and Medical Leave Act of 1993.
FOIA   Freedom of Information Act of 1966.
FPP   Fetal protection policy.
FSA   **1.** Family Support Act of 1988. **2.** Flexible spending account.
FUTA   Federal unemployment tax.
44   *See* Section 44, Internal Revenue Code.
401 (k)   *See* Section 401(k), Internal Revenue Code.

facilitator The person who is responsible for the *process* in any intervention, such as quality circles or training programs, but without the trappings of formal authority. Responsibility is exercised through persuasion rather than fiat. He or she serves as the teacher, trainer, instructor, moderator, coordinator, counselor, negotiator, ombudsman, marketer, advocate, and record keeper for the group or work team.

fact-finding An alternative dispute resolution procedure involving investigation of a dispute by a neutral third party who issues a report on the findings, usually recommending a basis for settlement. The report can also assist further negotiations between the parties involved. *See also* alternative dispute resolution procedure; expedited arbitration; mini-trial; rent-a-judge; summary jury trial.

fact-finding conference Informal meetings held under the auspices of the Equal Employment Opportunity Commission between the employer and the complainant in discrimination cases aimed at defining the issues and determining if there is a basis for negotiation.

However, in most cases the EEOC uses the conference as leverage to push for a settlement. *See also* conciliation.

factor analysis Methods of analyzing the interrelationships or intercorrelations among a set of variables, such as test scores. They are designed to identify the root "factors" that account for the interrelationships and determine how much of the variation is attributable to or associated with each of the factors.

factor comparison A quantitative method of job evaluation similar to job ranking. **Compensable factors** are selected for the jobs to be evaluated. All jobs are then placed in rank order on one of the compensable factors and are assigned a score reflecting their ranking. The process is continued for all compensable factors, one at a time. The scores are totaled for each job, resulting in a discrete job ranking or worth/value ranking. *See also* compensable factors; job classification; job evaluation; job ranking; point-factor method.

factor weight In **job evaluation,** a weight assigned to **compensable factors** to indicate relative importance. In a **point-factor** system, the factor weight is predetermined; for example, a firm may value experience twice as much as education and training and assign maximum values of 100 to experience and 50 to education.

Fair Credit Reporting Act of 1969 (FCRA) Regulates privacy and pre-employment checks and investigations. The Act protects candidates for employment by covering reports containing information on a person's character, general reputation, or life-style regardless of how it is obtained. If the prospective employer intends to use the information, the candidate must be advised in writing that such a report will be requested and also notified of his or her right to request information about the report. *See also* Freedom of Information Act of 1966; Privacy Act of 1974.

fair investigation A legal requirement that pertains to cases of unlawful discharge. It asks, "Was the employer's investigation of the violation considered and conducted fairly and objectively?"

Fair Labor Standards Act of 1938 (FLSA) The basic federal wage/hour legislation covering companies in interstate or foreign commerce. FLSA establishes and defines employee categories as exempt (compensation, usually salary, is exempt from the provisions of the Act) and nonexempt (wages are regulated by the Act). The Act and its amendments mandate a minimum wage and 40–hour workweek for employees of businesses engaged in interstate commerce who are nonexempt. It also establishes the principle of equal pay for equal work, right to time-and-a-half for hours worked in excess of the maximum (overtime pay), and prohibits the use of workers under the age of 16 in most jobs and under the age of 18 in hazardous jobs. The Act authorizes criminal prosecution for violations. The Department of Labor has jurisdiction. Also known as the *wages and hours law*. *See also* employee rights, right-to-work.

fair reimbursement law A state law that erects a barrier to **managed care** (currently on the books of 10 states). The law limits or prohibits differentials in payments to network and nonnetwork managed care providers, thereby forcing insurance carriers to limit the amount of network provider discounts. *See also* any willing-provider law; mandatory assignment.

False Claims Act Amendment of 1986 Legislation that permits any citizen who knows of a financial loss to the federal government from fraudulent activity to go directly to court and sue, in the name of the United States, to recover for the government an amount equal to three times the government's loss, plus a penalty of at least $5,000 for each act of fraud. Successful plaintiffs are entitled to keep up to 30 percent of the proceeds from such suits. The Act also gives full legal protection to an employee who files or cooperates with a *qui tam* suit from any form of retaliation on the job, including remedies of job reinstatement and damages doubling the amount of any pay lost due to any retaliatory treatment. *See also* whistleblower; Whistleblower Protection Act of 1989.

Family and Medical Leave Act of 1993 (FMLA) A bill that requires employers of 50 or more workers to provide up to 12 weeks of unpaid leave per year for childbirth, adoption of a child, or medical circumstances involving an employee or a close member of his or her family. The Act covers employees within a 75–mile radius and applies to nonprofit and government organizations as well as to businesses. Employees retain health benefits while on leave and must be reinstated in the same job or its equivalent upon return to work. Companies have the option of applying an employee's paid time off, including vacations and sick pay, toward their leave. Key employees, who constitute the highest-paid 10 percent of the work force, may be excluded. In states that require unpaid family leave, the most liberal law (state or federal) will apply. The law takes effect following the expiration of existing collectively bargained contracts or one year after the law's enactment, whichever comes first.

family care program (FCP) An alternative to nursing home care for the elderly and physically disabled established to provide a better quality of life and reduce costs. Care is provided by family members rather than professional health care providers. *See also* long-term care.

family day care network A form of direct employer-supported child care service in which employers contract with local agencies to recruit, train, and assist people to become licensed child care providers in their own homes. *See also* consortium child care center.

Family Support Act of 1988 (FSA) Includes the deadbeat dad provision. Focuses on establishing paternity and withholding wages for child support from fathers who fail to make child support payments mandated by the courts.

family support programs Programs offered by business, industry, community organizations, churches, schools, and youth-serving organizations to help parents balance their work and family responsibilities and compensate for damaging aspects of the social environment. Include family leave, job sharing, flexible schedules, part-time work, child care, home-visiting services, parent-child centers, life-skills training, mentoring, and self-help programs. *See also* flexible work options.

FASB Rule No. 106 A Financial Accounting Standards Board rule that was passed in 1991 and became effective December 15, 1992. The Rule requires large companies to pay and account for retirees' health insurance costs up front and acknowledge the future cost of the promise to pay for their retirees' medical claims. The Rule does not affect small companies until late 1994. Government employees are not affected. The Rule has caused some companies to eliminate health benefits for retirees to avoid listing the liability on their books. Others have cut or plan to cut retiree health benefits to limit their liability, resulting in higher deductibles and retirees' paying more for their health insurance.

fast-trackers Employees who have demonstrated exceptional promotion potential and are being groomed for higher-level jobs through coaching, training, and other forms of development.

featherbedding An unfair labor practice in which the union requires an employer to pay a worker for services not performed. *See* featherbed rule.

featherbed rule A union rule that requires an employer to create unneeded jobs, pay workers for duplicate services, guarantee a certain amount of overtime work, or adopt restrictive work rules, such as limiting the amount of work to be done in a day or week. *See* featherbedding.

Federal Insurance Contributions Act of 1935 (FICA) The Act is the source of Social Security and Medicare withholding requirements (the FICA pay deduction). The Act requires employers to pay the current percentage of the wage base and deduct an identical amount from the employee's pay, and remit the total to the federal government. It also requires employers to maintain records of all amounts paid to employees for services performed whether payment is in cash or other medium. *See also* Medicare; Social Security Act of 1935.

federal unemployment tax (FUTA) A tax paid by employers to the federal government to support payments to unemployed workers. It is currently 0.8 percent on the first $7,000 of income per employee.

fee-for-service plan or option A health benefits plan that pays benefits directly to physicians, hospitals, or other health care providers, or that reimburses the patient for covered medical services. Examples are Blue Cross & Blue Shield and Medicare.

fetal protection policy (FPP) A policy that excludes fertile women from jobs involving hazardous levels of exposure to solid, liquid, or gaseous toxic materials, such as lead, to prevent exposure of unborn fetuses to physical harm. *See also* fetal risk; Pregnancy Discrimination Act of 1978; Title VII.

fetal risk A matter ruled on by the Supreme Court in March 1991 (*United Auto Workers* v. *Johnson Controls*, manufacturer of automobile batteries). The case relates to whether an employer may legitimately exclude women of childbearing age from jobs that might expose them and the fetuses they may carry to dangerous levels of toxic substances, such as lead, glycol ethers, organic mercury (methyl), inorganic mercury, and radiation. The Court ruled that fetal protection is nothing more than an intrusive form of job discrimination. The decision stated, "It is no more appropriate for the courts than it is for individual employers to decide whether a woman's reproductive role is more important to herself and her family than her economic role. Congress has left this choice to the woman as hers to make." *See also* Civil Rights Act of 1964; fetal protection policy; Title VII.

fifty-fifty (50/50) dental plan A cost-cutting dental care plan that pays benefits of $1,000 orthodontic maximum, $1,000 annual maximum, but requires no deductibles.

financial assistance program (FAP) An employer-sponsored dependent care option. There are four types: flexible spending accounts, flexible benefits (salary reduction plans), voucher programs, and vendor programs.

fitness for work A document that contains information obtained from employer inquiries into a job applicant's background.

Five-Five-Five Plan (5-5-5 Plan) Attributed to futurist Alvin Toffler. A work proposal featuring a 25-hour workweek with five hours of training weekly, phased in over a five-year period. Designed to improve productivity, employee motivation, and job satisfaction.

fixed-dollar benefits Health care or other employee benefits plans in which specific dollar limitations are placed on the insurance premiums or claims paid by the company. *See also* employee prefunding; graduated benefits.

flagged rates Rates paid to employees which fall above the wage curve. Also called *red circle rates* or *overrates*.

flat benefit retirement plan A type of defined benefit pension plan that provides benefits that are unrelated to earnings, such as a certain amount per month or per year of service.

flexible benefits/flex benefits program (FBP) A program that allows employees to adjust their benefits to meet their needs. The employer decides how much money to allocate to benefits, medical for example, and the employee decides how to use those benefits. Such plans often feature less expensive core coverage options with varying deductibles and copayment requirements. Additional benefits may also be offered for purchase by the employee. *See also* cafeteria plan; paid time off; pooling.

flexible leave A plan for personal and parental paid, partially paid, or unpaid leave to allow employees to care for a new baby or for ill dependents.

flexible managed care A combination of a **cafeteria plan** and an **open-ended health maintenance organization** plan—adding managed care elements to their flexible benefits plans to make the plans more cost-effective.

flexible scheduling A plan to adjust employee schedules as needed to accommodate the business cycles or to increase employee motivation, morale, and job satisfaction.

flexible spending account (FSA) 1. A plan that allows employees to use pretax dollars to fund medical expenses not covered by their health plan (and sometimes dependent care). The only cost to the employer is for administrative expenses. Essentially a strategy to reduce health care costs, the plan is offered to employees instead of first-dollar coverage of hospitalization and surgery. A specific sum of money is put aside for each employee for prescription drugs and other outpatient services. The employer decides how much money to put toward benefits and the employee decides how to use that money—and may choose expenses not ordinarily covered by the employer. *See also* Section 125, Internal Revenue Code. **2.** An employer-sponsored dependent care option in which the employee chooses from a menu of taxable and nontaxable benefits. Dependent-care options are nontaxable. The dependent must be a child under 15, a dependent elderly relative, or a mentally or physically handicapped dependent.

flexible staffing A strategy designed to effect substantial savings in salaries and fringe benefits, reduce vulnerability to periodic or seasonal layoffs, and cut turnover. It involves the use of temporary full-time and permanent part-time personnel, consultants, and subcontractors, such as secretarial, accounting, technical, managerial, or executive-level employees.

flexible work options Optional schedules and alternative work sites designed to allow employees to balance work and family responsibilities. *See also* compressed workweek; family support programs; flexiplace; flextime; grandpa track; job sharing/job splitting; phased retirement; work sharing.

flexiplace An accommodation employers make to help their workers change their life-styles. Involves the performance of a job in whole or in part away from the company's premises—at home or elsewhere. *See also* compressed workweek; flexible work options; flextime; home worker; job sharing/job splitting; phased retirement; work sharing.

flex plans Cost-reduction strategies designed to transfer more of the costs of providing health care from the organization to employees.

flextime Arrangements made to allow flexibility in start and finish times of the work shift to accommodate employees whose day, hours, or family responsibilities do not match standard work hours. Employees are usually required to be present during "core" time—a set time for all employees. Also called *flexitime*. *See also* flexible work options; flexiplace.

formative evaluation An approach to the evaluation of training systems that focuses on the system's adequacy in terms of achievement of objectives. It also identifies corrections or changes needed in the system as it is being implemented. *See also* summative evaluation.

Form 5500 filings Annual reports to the Internal Revenue Service and the Department of Labor on qualified retirement plans due within seven months of the close of the plan's fiscal year. The reports cover such items as plan operations, level of employee participation, annual expenses, and information on the plan's investment portfolio. *See also* ERISA bond; summary annual report; summary plan description.

formulary drug A brand-name drug on a list of prescription drugs specifically approved for special benefit consideration after assessment of their value, efficacy, and utilization by a formulary committee, usually consisting of a group of physicians and pharmacologists. *See also* brand name drug; generic drug.

forward averaging A tax accounting technique that enables recipients of lump-sum retirement payments to pay taxes on these distributions as if they had been received over a specified period of time, beginning in the year of the distribution.

four-fifths rule A calculation prescribed by the Equal Employment Opportunity Commission to determine whether an employment practice has an **adverse impact** on protected groups. Adverse impact exists where a selection procedure results in hiring a protected group of applicants (African-Americans, for example) at a rate that is less than 80 percent of the rate for white applicants.

Freedom of Information Act of 1966 (FOIA) An act that provides for full and free disclosure to the public of information held by administrative agencies of the federal government. Exceptions are: where disclosure would cause harm to a governmental function, such as national defense or foreign policy; records relating to internal personnel rules and practices of a federal agency; personnel and medical files; properly classified national security information; privileged or confidential information such as trade secrets or confidential business information; audits of financial institutions; and law enforcement investigative materials. Records may be requested by private individuals or entities that are sufficiently particular to be identifiable, and they are not required to show need or purpose. Doubtful requests for information must be checked with a senior executive, lawyer, privacy officer, freedom-of-information officer, or public information officer. See *also* Fair Credit Reporting Act of 1969; Privacy Act of 1974.

front-end analysis Attributed to HRD Hall of Famer Joe Harless. A tool or technique used to improve human performance by diagnosing the causes of employee performance deficiencies and determining whether they are due to a lack of skills or knowledge that can be remedied by training or something else. It addresses performance problems by asking these questions: What are the indicators that a problem exists? What are the performance deficiencies revealed by the data? What is the relative value (in dollars) of solving the problem? *See also* job analysis; needs assessment.

G

GATB	General Aptitude Test Battery.
GAW	Guaranteed annual wage.
GBO	Gissel bargaining order.
GED	General education development.
GIC	Guaranteed investment contract.
GPA	Grade point average.
GPHMO	Group practice health maintenance organization.
GULP	Group universal life plan.

gain sharing A type of variable or incentive pay typically used to increase production by linking pay directly to specific improvements in a company's performance. Gain sharing is used primarily where quantitative levels of production are important measures of business success. Gains are shared with all employees in a unit monthly, quarterly, semiannually, or annually, according to a predetermined formula calculated on the value or gains of production over labor and other costs. A formula is used to monitor some performance variable such as productivity. Using the formula to measure gains over a targeted baseline, the company shares the resulting benefits with employees. The plan lets employees reap some of the rewards of their efforts based on teamwork and cooperation and by working harder and smarter. *See also* empowered profit sharing.

garnishment order An order issued by a court or other agency having legal jurisdiction that directs an agency (such as Social Security) or an employer to withhold a certain amount of benefits or pay each month and send them either to the court, agency, or other party, which then forwards them to the person or organization entitled to the payment (such as alimony or child support), or pay the stipulated amount directly to the entitled person or organization. States have established maximums, but in no case can federal maximums be exceeded.

gatekeeper An individual (such as a disability case manager) or group (such as a health care coalition) given responsibility for controlling costs by carefully managing a patient's therapy to minimize unnecessary or duplicative tests and treatment.

gay benefits The extension of heterosexual spousal benefits to homosexual couples.

General Aptitude Test Battery (GATB) A battery of tests used by about 35 state and 800 local offices of the U.S. Employment Service for prehiring selection and making referrals to businesses. The tests measure candidates' verbal, numerical, perceptual, and psychomotor skills.

general education development (GED) A test used to establish high school equivalency.

generic drug A drug that is sold under its chemical name. For example, ibuprofen is the generic name for Motrin. Generic drugs are required by law to meet the same standards of purity, effectiveness, and strength, and they are usually less expensive than their **brand name drug** counterparts. *See also* formulary drug.

Gissel bargaining order (GBO) A National Labor Relations Board directive that requires an employer to bargain with a union that has never won an election. Said to be a potential adverse consequence of a finding that an employee participation plan is unlawful. *See also* Electromation decision.

giveback A benefit, usually one with low monetary value, that the employer requires employees—whether in groups or unions—to surrender to achieve cost savings. Examples are Christmas parties, personalized stationery or notepads, magazine subscriptions, health club memberships, and use of company cars.

glass ceiling The bias barrier that keeps many women from advancing beyond middle management positions into the executive suite.

gold-collar workers Scientists, engineers, and other professional workers in short supply who are paid premium salaries to attract and retain them.

golden carrots Incentive programs that involve the use of such inducements to motivation and productivity as company stock, scholarships, all-expense-paid vacations, and "This Is Your Career" home videos.

golden handcuffs A means of retaining key employees. Incentives and benefits that are tied to continued employment with an organization. Termination of employment for any reason would result in forfeiture of the benefit or incentive.

golden handshake *See* early retirement incentive program.

golden parachute Lucrative severance salary and benefits contractual packages drawn up in advance and activated and awarded to senior executives upon a change in corporate control and at least one of several other triggering circumstances established by Congress in 1984. Examples are the official's subsequent termination without cause by the combined company, reduction in the official's responsibilities, or mandatory relocation. Benefits typically provide for an increase in or acceleration of payments or vesting or other rights of the employee. *See also* bronze parachute; tin parachute.

golden passport A master of business administration degree from a prestigious graduate school of business, which is often assumed to be the credential for high-level CEO/COO positions, high salaries, and perks.

good cause In union-management relations, a term often used to identify the standard by which employers must justify their disciplinary actions. *See also* just cause.

good faith effort strategy or system An approach to achieving results in affirmative action programs that involves changing policies and practices that have tended to contribute to the exclusion or underutilization of members of protected groups (minorities and females), such as advertising vacancies to reach minorities, providing child care services, and establishing basic skills programs. *See also* quota strategy or system.

government benefits program A benefits program supported by the federal government—although some are cooperative programs with state governments and many are administered by state public assistance offices. In addition to Social Security, other benefits programs include **Supplemental Security Income,** unemployment insurance, food stamps, child support enforcement, family and child welfare services, workers' compensation, veterans' benefits, railroad workers' retirement, help for the blind, and other special programs.

grade point average (GPA) An index of student achievement. It is calculated through the following steps: (1) multiply the grade point value (numerical grade awarded) by the number of credits for each course, (2) take the products of those multiplications and add them up; (3) add up the total number of credits, and (4) divide the sum of the products of the grade point values and credits by the sum of the credits.

graduated benefits Health care or other employee benefits plans in which the amount contributed by the employer is determined by the number of years the worker has been employed by the company, so shorter-term workers pay more for their coverage than those who have been with the company for many years. *See also* employee prefunding; fixed-dollar benefits.

grandpa track High-achieving, seasoned, and valued executives, senior managers, scientists, and engineers who have decided to leave the fast track and pursue a less stressful and more leisurely work pace and life-style. Companies have begun to accommodate these employees by implementing human resources policies to prevent them from leaving. Policies include elimination of responsibilities, **flexible work options,** home-based work, job engineering, sabbatical leaves, unpaid leave with full benefits, and personal leave. *See also* daddy track; mommy track.

granted entitlements Benefits given by Congress on the basis of need or for some other policy purpose, such as Aid to Dependent Children, food stamps, Medicaid, unemployment insurance, and farm subsidies. *See also* earned entitlements; entitlements.

graphic scale In performance evaluation, a rating scale that combines both numerical scales and adjectives (or descriptive phrases) that describe theoretically equally spaced degrees of performance placed below a horizontal line. The length of the line represents the full range of the ability, performance, or trait to be rated.

green training Training for executives and managers in environmental awareness. It is designed to educate personnel on the things they can do to become environmentally sensitive.

grid training An approach to team building developed by Blake and Mouton. Based on a "managerial grid" representing several possible leadership styles (depending upon whether the manager is more concerned with people or production), the four-phase program (which may extend over a period of three to five years) aims to develop 9,9 managers—people who are equally concerned about people and production.

grievance procedure A carefully worded description of the process to be followed by grievants, the union, and management in resolving grievances. The grievance procedure is made a part of the collective bargaining agreement or contract and contains the various steps (up to six or more), time limits for each step, and specific rules.

Griggs* v. *Duke Power A case tried before the U.S. Supreme Court in 1971 relating to the issue of employment tests, in which the Court stated that **Title VII** of the **Civil Rights Act of 1964** focused on the consequences of employment practices and not their intent. Although the Court criticized testing in general, it left companies free to use tests, but it banned tests that have an **adverse impact** on a **protected class** unless they can be demonstrated to be job-performance-related. *See also* Uniform Guidelines on Employee Selection Procedures.

group annuity An annuity that provides benefits to a group of plan participants under a single contract between the employer and the insurer. *See also* deferred annuity; variable annuity.

group auto insurance Employer-sponsored purchase of auto insurance referred to as mass merchandising by the insurance industry. The employer selects the insurance carrier and chooses an insurance agent to handle the enrollment. There are two forms: franchise group and true group programs. In the former, each employee is individually underwritten by the insurance company, pays individual premium rates, and receives an individual policy. With true group programs, participation is based on conditions relating to employment without individual underwriting. The employer selects the benefits, which are provided to all participants, and enters into a contract with the carrier. Participants are issued certificates.

group legal plan A type of benefit illegal in some states but supported by some large unions as a way of ensuring that their members will be able to protect their rights. Such plans provide employees with legal assistance with such problems as wills, divorce, accidents, purchasing a home, and traffic matters, supported in whole or in part by the employer.

group outplacement A cost-cutting approach to the provision of outplacement services to employees, including senior- and middle-level workers, who are losing their jobs because of corporate downsizing. Rather than individual counseling, employees are given assistance in small, goal-oriented groups. *See also* outplacement.

group pension plan A type of pension plan in which employers (and sometimes employees) make set contributions to a pension fund. *See also* deferred profit-sharing plan; savings plan.

group practice health maintenance organization (GPHMO) An HMO that contracts with teams of multidisciplinary physicians in private practice who agree to provide health care to plan members, often in collaboration with their continuing private practices. GPHMOs deliver a wide range of services at one location and provide inpatient services through affiliated hospitals. *See also* health maintenance organization; network and mixed model health maintenance organization; staff model health maintenance organization.

group universal life plan (GULP) An extension of group universal life insurance that combines term protection for beneficiaries with an investment element for the policyholder. Such plans are financed by employees' after-tax payroll deduction contributions. Excess contributions may go into an investment fund that earns on a tax-deferred basis, and earnings can be used to pay premiums. Participation is entirely voluntary.

guaranteed annual income Consists of payments made by an employer when a plant must be shut down for equipment repair or replacement and is in addition to unemployment benefits. *See also* supplemental unemployment benefits.

guaranteed annual wage (GAW) A compensation plan that guarantees a minimum annual income to employees.

guaranteed investment contract (GIC) A type of defined benefit plan issued by life insurance companies. A GIC is a funding plan vehicle for annuity contracts. GICs pay a fixed interest rate on a specified deposit for a defined period of time (typically one to six years) and most are carried under book value. Benefits-responsive GICs permit employees who are eligible for a distribution from their plans to withdraw their investments at book value before the contract reaches maturity without taking any market value adjustment. It is possible that FASB accounting standards for other **defined benefit plans** (fair market value as the appropriate method of valuation for defined benefit plans) may be applied to 401(k) plans. As of this writing, however, GICs are the overwhelming choice for 401(k) accounts because employees fear volatility and seek a higher return than money market funds provide. *See also* defined benefit plan; deposit administration arrangement.

guaranteed piecework plan A piece-rate plan in which employees are guaranteed a minimum hourly wage regardless of the number of items they process or produce.

H

HCE	Highly compensated employee.
HCS	Hazard Communication Standard of 1988.
HFE	Human factors engineering.
HIPC	Health insurance purchasing cooperative.
HMO	Health maintenance organization.
HMOA	Health Maintenance Organization Acts of 1973 and 1988.
HPO	Health care purchasing organization.
HR	Human resources.
HRA	Human resources accounting.
HRD	Human resources development.
HRIS	Human resources information system.
HRM	Human resources management.

hardship premium A monthly payment, typically a percentage of base pay, paid to employees assigned to areas in which unusual or environmental hazards exist.

Hay plan A method of job evaluation that focuses on job incumbents' job knowledge and skills, problem-solving abilities, and responsibility and accountability as **compensable factors**.

Hazard Communication Standard of 1988 (HCS) An OSHA requirement aimed at reducing the incidence of chemical-related occupational illnesses and injuries in nonmanufacturing workplaces. The regulation requires employers of even one employee in any type of enterprise to establish hazard communication plans and programs to transmit information on the hazards of chemicals to their employees by means of labels on containers, publication and distribution of materials safety data sheets, and conduct of training programs. Also known as the **right-to-know** standard. *See also* Bloodborne Pathogens Standard; Comprehensive Environmental Response, Compensation, and Liability Act of 1980; Confined Spaces Standard; Laboratory Chemical Standard; Superfund Amendments and Reauthorization Act of 1986.

health care purchasing organization (HPO) A form of managed health care. HPOs are employer-sponsored purchasing groups organized to buy health care directly from providers (hospitals, physicians, and other professionals) rather than going through **health maintenance organizations** (HMOs) or **preferred provider organizations.**

health care reimbursement account An option under a flexible benefits plan. Expenses paid for uninsured medical, vision, hearing, and dental expenses (such as deductibles, copayments/coinsurance, exams, and the like) are reimbursable by the employer on a nontaxable basis provided that rules established by the Internal Revenue Service are met. *See also* day care reimbursement account; reimbursement account.

health insurance purchasing cooperative (HIPC) A state-based agency that arranges insurance for business and individuals under **managed competition plans.** HIPCs may also enforce spending ceilings and limit premium increases.

health maintenance organization (HMO) A privately established organization qualified by state or federal agencies to offer its services to employees and employers in a specified geographical area. Subscribers who elect to participate in HMOs in preference to employer-sponsored health insurance programs are entitled to a subsidy to their HMO premiums equal to the amount they would otherwise be subsidized under the company plan. Programs provide prepaid routine, round-the-clock medical services at a specific site and usually stress preventive medicine in a clinic. Costs to enrolled employees are limited to a nominal fee, and the charges of medical care providers to the employer are on a prenegotiated, fixed annual payment per employee basis. *See also* competitive medical plan; group practice health maintenance organization; open-ended health maintenance organization; preferred provider organization.

Health Maintenance Organization Act of 1973 (HMOA) An Act designed to stimulate a nationwide, prepaid health care system. The HMOA required employers to offer local HMO coverage to employees if the employer is approached by a qualified HMO—a medical organization consisting of several specialists, such as general practitioners, surgeons, psychiatrists, and so on.

Health Maintenance Organization Act of 1988 (HMOA) Legislation mandating a new group-specific rating plan that allows HMOs to set rates based on specific group utilization (similar to the way indemnity insurers set rates); extends the dual choice mandate, which forces employers of 25 or more workers to offer both an indemnity

or HMO plan until 1995; and renews the equal contribution for indemnity or HMO plans.

highly compensated employee (HCE) A term standardized by the **Tax
Reform Act of 1986** that is used to test for discrimination. At this
time, HCEs are considered to be employees who are 5 percent owners, all those earning more than $75,000 from the employer, all
those earning more than $50,000 from the employer and in the top-
paid 20 percent, any officer earning more than $45,000, or one of
the top-ten highest-paid employees of the employer. *See also* non-
highly-compensated employee.

high-performance jobs Jobs that rely on worker problem solving, place
heavy emphasis on training to upgrade skills, require cooperation
between labor and management, and involve the integration of
technology into the production process. Proposed as a strategy to
help industry and unions survive in a world of intense global competition. Attributed to Secretary of Labor Robert Reich at the Conference on the Future of the American Workplace in Chicago in July
1993.

high-technology training (hi-tech training) Developing and delivering
training on leading-edge technologies and evolving processes for
technical professionals, scientists, and engineers. It aims to reduce
product development time and speed up technology transfer. Examples: the use of computers, telecommunications, interactive
video, optical discs, CD-ROM, laser discs, digital video interactive,
EXPERT systems, and the like to deliver training.

home health care Health services (such as nursing services and rehabilitative therapy) and supplies provided to a covered individual on a
part-time, intermittent, or visiting basis in the person's home while
he or she is confined due to injury, disease, or pregnancy. Usually
a physician must certify that the services and supplies are provided
as an alternative to admission to a hospital or skilled nursing facility. May be covered in part by **Medicare, Medicaid,** and **medigap
insurance.** *See also* hospice care.

home leave A periodic leave (usually annual) in the United States (or
country of domicile) for employees and their dependents assigned
overseas.

home marketing assistance A relatively new employee benefit instituted to reduce the spiraling costs of relocating employees: purchasing the transferee's home, paying all home sale expenses, covering
the cost of finding a home in the destination area, and transporting
the family and household goods to the new location.

home purchase company An organization established to help transferring employees get the equity out of their old homes as fast as pos-

sible so they can move to the new location and settle in without worrying about their property. Such companies buy the property.

home sale protection A benefit for relocated and expatriate employees that pays the costs associated with selling a house to take an assignment either overseas or in another geographical area of the United States. If the employee elects not to sell the property, the company may offer home rental protection that provides some property management services and reimburses employees for extraordinary expenses (for example, credit checks) associated with the rental or lease.

home worker An employee who performs his or her duties at a location away from the plant, shop, or office. A Department of Labor rule allows DOL-certified employers to employ home workers (they had formerly been banned because of the difficulties in enforcing labor standards). Recently the authorization to employ home workers was extended to the knitted outerwear, gloves and mittens, buttons and buckles, handkerchiefs, embroidery, and nonhazardous jewelry industries. *See also* flexiplace; work sharing.

honesty test A substitute for polygraph examinations. Honesty tests make use of pencil-and-paper tests or projective techniques as a part of an applicant screening and selection process to identify persons with tendencies to be dishonest. A study conducted by the U.S. Office of Technology Assessment in 1990 determined that existing research is inconclusive as to whether or not honesty and integrity tests accurately predict dishonest workplace behavior.

hospice care Programs operated by a licensed or accredited public agency or private organization that engages primarily in providing pain relief, symptom management, and supportive services for terminally ill people and their families. Such programs typically combine acute inpatient, outpatient, and home care for the patient as well as grief or bereavement counseling for his or her family. *See also* home health care.

hospital An institution that is licensed, provides 24–hour-per-day medical and nursing care, and has facilities for diagnosis and major surgery. The term may also be used to describe a licensed ambulatory surgical center or a facility operated by a hospice or one that provides inpatient care under arrangements made by a hospice.

hospital confinement indemnity coverage An insurance policy that pays a fixed amount for each day that a subscriber is confined to a hospital, up to a specified maximum number of days.

housing allowance A differential paid to employees to adjust for differences, including both rent and basic utilities, between housing costs overseas and comparable housing in the United States.

HR strategic plan Management's vision of what the corporation's human needs and requirements will be in the future and what the HR organization must become to meet those needs.

human factors engineering (HFE) Systematic and controlled study and research to adapt the work environment and human tasks to the sensory, perceptual, mental, physical, and esthetic attributes, capacities, and preferences of people. HFE is concerned with workplace layout, equipment controls, instrument design, furniture and furnishings, and environmental conditions (lighting, noise level, and so on).

human resources (HR) **1.** The people that staff and operate an organization—the executives, managers, supervisors, scientists and engineers, technicians, marketing and sales personnel, administrative and clerical personnel, and hourly workers—as contrasted with the financial and material resources of an organization. **2.** The organizational function that deals with the people who manage, produce, market, and sell the products and services of an organization.

human resources accounting (HRA) A means of measuring employees' costs and value to an organization. A tool to help management make decisions based on facts, figures, and historical data in matters such as hiring, layoffs, transfers, training, and retaining people. Typically performed by the accounting department in conjunction with the HR or personnel department.

human resources development (HRD) Career development, training and development, and organization development programs offered to employees to develop new or replacement knowledge and skills, improve their performance, potential, and promotability, enhance their general personal growth, and improve group and overall organizational effectiveness. *See also* education; organization development.

human resources information system (HRIS) A computer-based system for collecting, storing, maintaining, and retrieving data on people, jobs, compensation and benefits, and employment forecasts and conditions to automate HR functions and provide data to managers on demand. Also known as *human resources management system, human resources system,* and *personnel system.*

human resources management (HRM) The organization function that focuses on the management and direction of people. HRM deals with the human element in the organization—people as individuals and groups, their recruitment, selection, assignment, motivation, compensation, utilization, services, training, development, promotion, termination, and retirement.

I

ICM	Individual case management.
ILS	Integrated learning system.
IMAC 90	Immigration Act of 1990.
INA	Immigration and Nationality Act of 1952.
IRA	Individual retirement account.
IRCA	Immigration Reform and Control Act of 1986.
ISD	Instructional systems development.
ISO	Incentive stock options.

icebreaker An opener, warm-up, energizer, and tension-reducer for training sessions and workshops, such as a game or brain-teaser. Icebreakers help the trainer or workshop leader begin sessions with impact, acquaint participants with one another comfortably, and re-energize group members during flat periods.

immediate evaluation Evaluation that focuses on ongoing programs and activities. Its objective is to assess the quality of programs and services while they are in operation to provide supervisors and employees or instructors and trainees the feedback they need to improve their performance. There are three subcategories of immediate evaluation: participant reaction, measurement of behavioral or attitudinal change, and the self-evaluation or self-audit. *See also* intermediate evaluation; ultimate evaluation.

Immigration Act of 1990 (IMAC 90) Legislation that reconstructed the controlling immigration statutes. Most employment-related provisions of the law went into effect October 1, 1991. The Act includes a new classification and quota system for the allocation of immigrant visas (for temporary workers) and affects all persons seeking permanent residency status in the United States. One of the most significant features of the Act is that persons seeking entry on the basis of an offer of employment from a U.S. employer may do so as long as they present unique expertise, training, and experience. It creates a separate category for professionals (such as engineers, scientists, accountants, health practitioners, and teachers) with advanced degrees and gives them priority over lesser-skilled workers.

Immigration and Nationality Act of 1952 (INA) An Act that made it unlawful for any person or organization to hire, recruit, or refer for a fee, an alien for employment in the United States, knowing the alien is unauthorized for employment or, after hiring an alien authorized employment, continuing to employ that individual knowing that the alien has become unauthorized with respect to employment. The Act also deals with the admission and employment of special agricultural workers and temporary workers and proscribes discrimination against aliens authorized employment on the basis of national origin or citizenship status.

Immigration Reform and Control Act of 1986 (IRCA) Designed to stem the influx of illegal immigrants, the Act instituted a system of penalties for employers or referral agencies who knowingly recruit, hire, or refer illegal aliens. Employers must file INS form I–9, Employment Eligibility Verification Form, certifying that all newly hired employees are not illegal aliens by ascertaining that they have a U.S. passport, a certificate of U.S. citizenship, a certificate of naturalization, a resident alien card, or a combination of documents (such as Social Security and birth certificates) showing authorization to work in the United States.

impact evaluation An approach to evaluation that focuses on the effects (bottom-line results) of programs on individuals or departments, divisions, or corporations. Examples are the extent to which a wellness program reduced absenteeism and accidents or the extent to which an executive succession program, coupled with a cross-cultural training program, provided the executives needed for a global expansion program. *See also* context evaluation; justification evaluation; needs assessment.

implacement Helping workers whose jobs have been abolished to identify new career interests and options and develop the skills needed to fulfill them. May involve testing, assessment, career counseling, and retraining. Sometimes undertaken to avoid the costs of recruiting and training new employees. *See also* redeployment.

in-basket exercise An instructional method (also used as an assessment center evaluative device) involving the use of a representative sample of a month's or even a full year's performance in all aspects of a job. It is used to analyze and evaluate trainees' decision-making abilities or to provide practice in decision making. Trainees are given background materials and are then exposed to a structured array of memos, reports, letters, telephone calls, visits, and meetings. In the role of manager, the trainee makes decisions on the incoming "mail." Time limits are established to introduce realism and cause stress. The decision-making phase is followed by discussion and critiques of the actions taken and decisions reached. All actions are analyzed, evaluated, and fed back to participants. *See also* analysis exercise; assessment center; job sampling.

incentive plan A plan that provides financial rewards to workers whose productivity or contributions to the organization exceed some predetermined standard. Incentives for production workers include piecework plans and group incentive plans; for executives and managers, bonuses, stock options, and the like; for salespersons, commissions, bonuses, and special awards. *See also* deferred compensation; merit rating.

incentive retirement plan Incentives offered to encourage early retirement, used as a painless method of reducing personnel during downsizing and restructuring. They involve enhancement of earned retirement benefits and are paid to all eligible employees who volunteer to retire during the period in which the program is offered.

incentive stock options (ISO) Authorized by the Economic Recovery Act of 1981, an ISO grants an employee, usually an executive, the right to pay the current market price for shares in the company at a future time. ISOs qualify for favorable tax treatment under Section 422A, Internal Revenue Code.

incentive work Used where work output is measurable in units of product, pieces, items, and so on, and the rate of pay is stated as dollars paid for each unit or piece produced. Also called *piece rate; piecework.*

in-company diagnosis A form of employee assistance program. The practice of hiring a professional to diagnose the problems of employees and then to refer them to appropriate external sources of help. Also called *in-house diagnosis. See also* referral agent program.

in-country support An intercultural intervention in which persons assigned overseas are provided specific contacts and help of all kinds on an as-needed basis for the first three or four months of the foreign assignment.

indemnity plan 1. An insurance plan that offers protection against loss or damages, current or future, by providing compensation or remuneration for losses sustained. 2. In medical and health benefits, typically a benefit provided by an insurance company and which constitutes a plan, such as a major medical plan, that reimburses an employee for "usual and customary" medical expenses in excess of a deductible of $100 a calendar year, 80 percent of the next $5,000, and 100 percent above that amount, and sometimes limited to a semiprivate hospital room.

independent contractor As distinguished from an **employee** by the Internal Revenue Service, a person who works for wages or a salary and whose labor and how it is performed is largely determined by the worker and not the employer. The IRS uses a 20-point test to make the distinction. The consequence is a difference in the employer's tax liability. For employees, the employer must pay a 7.7 percent Social Security tax for the first $57,600 of employee income and a federal unemployment tax of 6.2 percent for the first $7,000 of compensation. Independent contractors must pay their own taxes. State taxes also add to the costs of "employees."

individual case management (ICM) Monitoring and influencing the treatment of employees with personal, social, or emotional problems.

individual incentive A type of compensation or pay-for-performance plan that ties all or a part of an employee's pay to his or her own performance. It is particularly appropriate where individual output is measurable and quantifiable.

individual retirement account (IRA) A form of defined contribution plan and an inducement to savings and investment. IRAs permit deferral of taxes (and in some cases are tax deductible) on income placed in retirement accounts to be incrementally withdrawn at a later date (withdrawals must begin before the age of 70½) when taxes are to be paid. To qualify, deferrals are prescribed in terms of annual limits, withdrawal restrictions, and penalties. Recent changes to tax laws severely restrict tax-free IRAs. *See also* rollover.

industrial rehabilitation Programs and therapies designed to get employees back on the job as soon as possible following accidents or injuries and reduce expenditures for compensation claims. *See also* work hardening.

insourcing Administering benefit plans, such as flexible benefits, internally. Permits valuable access to and control of data. Also advantageous when consulting firms and service bureaus cannot support the employer's objectives or do not run on the company's existing computer system. Sophisticated software applications are available commercially for most minicomputer and mainframe computer platforms. *See also* outsourcing.

institutional partnerships Contractual partnerships established by organizations and area technical schools, colleges, and universities to develop programs, including undergraduate and graduate degree programs, tailored to the needs and requirements of the organization. The institution and the corporation jointly determine enrollment requirements, plan and develop the curriculum, and establish course or degree completion standards and requirements. The school, college, or university provides the instructors (although some courses may be taught by employees of the corporation), and organizes and administers the program. Courses may be conducted either on the premises of the corporation or at the institution—or both. *See also* tuition-aid program.

instructional method The basic approach to instruction used. Examples are lecture, conference, demonstration, performance, individual study, programmed instruction, case studies, and simulation. *See also* instructional strategy; instructional technique.

instructional strategy The combination of methods of teaching, mediating devices, and the system of organizing trainees and instructors to accomplish an instructional objective. Selection of strategy is based on the learning objectives, the nature of the subject matter or content, the trainee population, the number, quality, experience, and competencies of the instructional staff, and availability of space, facilities, equipment, materials, time, and costs. *See also* instructional method; instructional technique; method.

instructional systems development (ISD) A rigorous, systematic model for developing instructional systems that was initiated by the Armed Services in the early 1970s. It consists of five phases: analysis, design, development, implementation, and evaluation.

instructional technique A means of instruction that complements a method; for example, questioning, handling trainee responses, and using visual and auditory aids. *See also* instructional method; instructional strategy.

instruction sheet A variation of the job procedures manual, instruction sheets provide written or printed directions to workers on a single sheet of paper. They typically cover a single task, and may accompany a piece of equipment to explain how to operate it, or a set of directions written for a temporary employee. *See also* job aids.

instructor-to-trainee ratio A common instructional standard, often established in the collective bargaining agreement. It is the maximum number of trainees that can be assigned to one instructor expressed as a ratio, such as 1:25.

integrated learning system (ILS) A unit of sequenced courseware complemented with management software delivered by networked computers. The courseware addresses a specific content area, and the software provides tracking and reporting capabilities. ILSs are designed to deliver networked-managed instruction. Several manufacturers are now experimenting with CD-ROM technology, and others offer the ability to incorporate different hardware platforms into the same network. Still others give instructors complete control of every aspect of ILS, allowing them to choose exactly which activity is delivered to trainees.

intelligence test A test that measures learning or problem-solving ability, which may be administered in written, oral, or nonverbal form. Intelligence tests are used in screening and selection, promotion, and training and development. Examples are tests of general mental ability (Wonderlic Personnel Test, Adaptability Test, Weschler Adult Intelligence Scale, and the Thurston Test of Mental Alertness) and tests of specific mental abilities (such as the Differential Aptitude Test and the Armed Forces Standard Aptitude Battery).

interactive performance system On-demand training and learner-controlled training. Computer-driven systems designed to support workers at the job site by providing assistance when needed. *See also* performance support system.

intercultural training Training provided by intercultural and multicultural organizations, public and private institutions and agencies, and the military services. It is provided to increase managerial effectiveness in international operations, negotiations, and decision making, help employees adapt to working, living, and learning environments in cultural settings different from their own, and establish friendly, cooperative, and favorable relationships with the people of a host country or culture. *See also* cross-cultural training.

intermediate evaluation Assessment of trainees' reactions, learning, and performance at the conclusion of training. The evaluation may take either of two forms: individual or organizational. Individual evaluation examines changes in on-the-job behavior of managers, supervisors, workers, clients, or customers, usually following training, development, or other form of intervention. Techniques include questionnaires, rating scales, interviews, tests, and observation. Organizational evaluation examines organizational change in such areas as quality of communications, customer relations, job satisfaction, motivation and morale, and teamwork. Tools include observation, questionnaires, interviews, ratings, and review of records. *See also* immediate evaluation; ultimate evaluation.

Interpretative Guidelines on Sexual Harassment Issued by the Equal Employment Opportunity Commission in March 1980, the guidelines detail employers' responsibilities for maintaining a workplace free of sexual harassment and intimidation.

investigation A legal doctrine that pertains to unlawful discharge. It asks, "Did the employer, before administering the disciplinary action, make an effort to find out whether the employee violated a rule or an order?"

J

JPA   Job performance aid.
JPM   Job performance measure.
JTPA   Job Training Partnership Act of 1982.

job The duties and tasks that a single worker performs. The basic unit used by personnel to carry out the actions of screening, selecting, classifying, training, assigning, developing, and promoting employees. Examples of a job are electronic equipment repairer and plant superintendent. *See also* duty; element; task.

job aids Materials that provide step-by-step directions for performing specific technical tasks to reduce training time, error rates, and dependence on instructors. They may be in paper (document or manual), computerized, or visual (slides, motion picture, or videocassette) form. *See also* instruction sheet.

job analysis The process of collecting, tabulating, grouping, analyzing, interpreting, and reporting data pertaining to the work performed by individuals who fill operative, clerical, technical, staff, supervisory, or managerial positions. Job analysis focuses on the duties, tasks, and elements that make up a job. The results of job analyses are used to identify and organize content for writing and revising **job descriptions** and **applicant specifications;** provide detailed job data that can be used to identify personnel requirements resulting from installation of new equipment, tools, work methods, or processes, and from development of new products and services; project future personnel requirements resulting from restructuring or downsizing; establish accurate and objective information for job evaluation; provide guidance for decisions relating to compensation and benefits, assignment and transfer, on-the-job training and development, and promotion; aid in the development of more effective recruitment, screening, selection, assignment, and classification instruments and procedures; establish measurable job performance standards; identify factors that induce job satisfaction, raise morale, and improve productivity; identify and locate health and safety hazards; and design training and development systems. *See also* front-end analysis; job inventory; task analysis.

job bank A means of compensating for the loss of employees with essential skills. Job banks enroll retired employees for temporary and part-time positions on an "as needed" basis.

job classification A method of job evaluation that involves segregating all jobs in an organization into occupational groups, establishing and defining a series of levels within each group (noting required standards pertaining to knowledge and skills, training and experience, accountability and responsibility, and so on), and finally matching each job to the appropriate level described in the standards. The result is a series of classifications within each occupational group that are not necessarily comparable or equivalent from one group to another. *See also* compensable factors; factor comparison; job evaluation; job ranking; point-factor method.

job description A document that describes the major duties, functions, and authority assigned to a position and the relationships between the position and other positions in the department, and, when appropriate, the relationship of that job to positions in other departments. It is one of the main products of **job analysis.** *See also* applicant specifications; job dimensions.

job design The process of developing or redeveloping the parameters of a job by identifying major functions, duties, and tasks, describing the relationships of the job to other positions in the organization, and documenting them in a written job description. *See also* job enrichment.

job displacement Job elimination regardless of whether the incumbent is terminated or transferred. *See also* displacement; employment displacement.

job engineering A performance management technique or intervention in which the job is changed in some way—made more simple, more challenging, more interesting—to promote employee productivity. *See also* job enrichment.

job enrichment Redesigning jobs to motivate people to work to their capacity and level of ability, improve employee morale, job satisfaction, and commitment to the organization, remedy performance shortfalls or problems, develop employee skills and abilities, make accommodations for employees with disabilities, and prevent employee dissatisfaction, grievances, slowdowns, and strikes. *See also* job design; job engineering.

job evaluation A means of comparing jobs to establish their relative level, importance, and value in the organizational scheme of things, including the remuneration that will be allotted, usually resulting in a schedule of position grades or a hierarchy of classifications. *See also* benchmarks; compensable factors; factor comparison; job classification; job ranking; point-factor method; wage curve.

job fair A cost-effective recruitment strategy. Several companies within a geographical area share advertising and site rental costs to stage an employment effort designed to attract candidates for positions as well as identify employment and salary trends and changes in the labor market.

job grade A class or group into which jobs of comparable value are placed for compensation purposes. Typically, all jobs at a given grade have the same pay range.

job lock Employees who remain in a job they really want to leave to keep their current health benefits and not chance any break in their eligibility for those benefits. Job lock is evidence of the growing concern about the costs of medical insurance and health care and the increasing numbers of employers who are reducing benefits costs by using cost-sharing strategies.

job performance aid (JPA) A document or printed guide that does not have to be committed to memory. It is provided to employees for use on the job. Examples are manuals, charts, tables, and checklists.

job performance counseling A manager-initiated strategy for improving employee efficiency, effectiveness, and productivity to achieve job adjustment, improve motivation and morale, decrease absenteeism, reduce turnover, foster acceptance of change, release emotional tension, reduce stress, and promote teamwork. It lets employees know where they stand, what they do well, where they are deficient, and how they can improve. *See also* developmental counseling.

job performance measure (JPM) A test or other evaluative instrument that provides the basis for developing training systems and controlling their quality. JPMs define and describe the job-related outcomes the training should produce. *See also* criterion measure.

job posting Internal or external advertising and recruiting for current position vacancies. Postings include listing the duties, authority, qualifications, supervision received, work schedule, and pay rate. *See also* bidding.

job pricing The process of determining the appropriate rate of pay or salary for a specific job with due consideration for prevailing industry and regional rates as determined by systematic wage and salary surveys. *See also* benchmarks.

job ranking The simplest method of job evaluation. All jobs in an organization are ranked by a knowledgeable person or group (usually managers or supervisors) in order of their perceived importance and worth to the organization. *See also* compensable factors; factor comparison; job classification; job evaluation; point-factor method.

job-relatedness An important legal concept that requires employers to demonstrate that an action, requirement, or program is directly related to the job. Job-relatedness is only raised as a consideration when an employer's objection to an employee's refusal to comply with direction is based on protected grounds. *See also* protected characteristics.

job replica test A behavioral simulation used to test for abilities required by the types of tasks that must be performed in the target job; for example, a driving test for a delivery service; a typing test for a secretarial position.

job rotation An informal method of training and development, often used in conjunction with coaching. Job rotation is a technique whereby potential managers receive diversified training and experience under close supervision through rotation for specified periods of time in nonsupervisory or managerial jobs, observational assignments, or training or assistant-to positions. It is designed to improve employees in their present jobs and prepare them for future positions. In some cases, managers are rotated through all major departments in an organization for one month each.

job sampling A technique used in employee selection that involves observing or measuring how an applicant actually performs some of the basic tasks of a job. *See also* assessment center; in-basket exercise.

job sharing/job splitting An arrangement that allows employees to fulfill their job responsibilities and provide more time for them to care for their dependents by dividing a job and the workday or workweek between two part-time employees. For example, one employee may work from 8:00 A.M. to 12:00 P.M. and the other from 1:00 P.M. to 5:00 P.M.; or one employee may work Mondays, Wednesdays, and Fridays and the other Tuesdays and Thursdays. There is a distinction, however, between job sharing and job splitting. Job sharing involves two employees whose duties overlap, think of each other as an extension of themselves, and therefore must communicate. Their shifts may overlap to facilitate such communication, but it is not an essential feature because they may communicate by E-mail or less sophisticated means, such as periodic meetings, phone calls, or notes. Job splitting involves creating two clearly distinct, separate, and independent jobs from one job. No communication between incumbents is needed. *See also* flexible work options; flexiplace; work sharing.

Job Training Partnership Act of 1982 (JTPA) The federal government's largest job-skills training program, targeted at educationally disadvantaged and displaced youths and adults, especially women, minorities, disabled, disadvantaged, disabled veterans, veterans of the Vietnam era, and veterans recently separated from military service. It funnels federal training funds to the states for local use. The Act replaces CETA, the Comprehensive Employment and Training Act of 1973. The legislation requires states to establish Service Delivery Areas (SDAs), local areas in which JTPA services are developed, implemented, and provided. SDAs provide such services as client assessment, basic education and remediation services, job training, and placement services free of change for all JTPA participants. JTPA Title II serves economically disadvantaged individuals. Title III is directed specifically at dislocated workers. The Act also allows employers a 50 percent wage reimbursement of the first six months of employment for disabled individuals who meet established economic guidelines.

joint-activities staff Members of the staff paid by both union and management to patrol assembly lines and oversee work teams, cultivate cooperation, and identify opponents of union-management unity and meddlers or obstructionists of union elections. Also called *thought police.*

just cause Legal terminology used in connection with termination or discharge of an employee. To protect itself against litigation, management must ensure that it has enforced its rules consistently, that it has made a fair, thorough, and impartial investigation of the facts in the case, that there are credible witnesses to the offense, and the penalty for the offense is fair under the circumstances. Seven tests apply: reasonableness, adequate notice, investigation, fairness, adequacy of proof, equal treatment, and appropriate penalty. *See also* good cause.

justification evaluation The form of evaluation most commonly used in the HR field. It involves the collection of evidence to prove the need for initial, continued, or increased funding and other support for programs, services, and activities. Evidence usually takes the form of documentation showing that the programs, services, or activities are effective, save time and money, improve productivity and performance, and so forth. *See also* impact evaluation; needs assessment.

K

K&R   Kidnap and ransom (insurance).

Keogh Plan A plan that gives a self-employed individual, under strict IRS rules and requirements, the option to establish a qualified tax-deductible pension or profit-sharing plan. Also known as an *H.R. 10 Plan.*

key contributor program A compensation plan used to recognize and reward individuals or teams whose skills, abilities, performance, or contributions have improved or will significantly improve an organization's products, services, or processes and thereby improve market position, productivity, or profitability.

key-man insurance An insurance policy that can be combined with a nonqualified deferred compensation arrangement when the employer needs both financial protection against the loss of a key employee through death and adequate additional retirement income for the employee in the event that he or she survives a serious accident, injury, or illness and returns to work.

kidnap and ransom (K&R) insurance Insurance coverage provided by some companies for their employees who work in areas where there is the possibility of their being taken as hostages by terrorists or maverick governments. Such policies are written on a worldwide basis, and currently there are no restricted areas. Coverage provides for payment of ransom expenses and sometimes includes coverage for lost income. K&R may also provide the services of a protection consultant who can assist a company to avoid difficult situations and respond appropriately to a crisis.

kiosk A computer-based interactive system installed in corporate cafeterias and work areas to perform a range of functions such as accessing general information about benefits, checking the status of savings plans, making calculations of benefits coverage, and changing the mix of benefits in a flexible benefit program.

L

LBR	Living benefits rider.
LMRA	Labor-Management Relations Act of 1947.
LMRDA	Labor-Management Reporting and Disclosure Act of 1959.
LSD	Lump sum distribution.
LTC	Long-term care.

Laboratory Chemical Standard Regulations issued by the Occupational Safety and Health Administration to minimize or eliminate exposure to hazardous chemicals in laboratories. The Standard requires lab operators to train their workers in chemical safety and develop a chemical hygiene plan. *See also* Bloodborne Pathogens Standard; Confined Spaces Standard; Hazard Communication Standard of 1988.

labor demand The highest wage or salary employers are willing to pay for a specific level of employment or number of employees.

labor law posting Federal regulations require four specific Equal Employment Opportunity labor law posters as of July 26, 1992. Random inspections will be made by the EEOC and the Occupational Safety and Health Administration to ensure compliance. The posters must cover equal employment opportunity rights under the **Equal Employment Opportunity Act of 1972** and the **Americans with Disabilities Act of 1990,** federal minimum wage rights under the **Fair Labor Standards Act of 1938** and the Amendments of 1990, job safety and health protection under the **Occupational Safety and Health Act of 1970,** and polygraph protection under the Employee Polygraph Protection Act of 1988. *See also* state employment postings.

labor-management contract An agreement reached in good faith by negotiators representing a labor union and management and legally binding on both parties. Labor-management contracts contain the following: (1) definition of recognition and representation of the un-

91

ion as the exclusive bargaining agent for employees and the jobs or categories of jobs included and excluded; (2) requirements for union membership and termination of membership; (3) wage rates and methodology for job evaluation, rate changes and adjustments, transfers, upgrading and downgrading, and incentive plans, and extent of participation of the union in the foregoing items; (4) management rights; (5) union rights; and (6) union proscriptions. Also known as *collective bargaining agreements. See also* collective bargaining.

Labor-Management Relations Act of 1947 (LMRA) An amendment to the **National Labor Relations Act of 1935** (Wagner Act), LMRA proscribed certain union activities and thereby balanced laws that had placed responsibility for unfair labor practices mainly on employers. The Act prohibited unfair labor practices, enumerated the rights of employees as union members, enumerated the rights of employers, and allowed the President of the United States to temporarily bar national emergency strikes. The law also created the Federal Mediation and Conciliation Service. Also known as the *Taft-Hartley Act. See also* Taft-Hartley Amendment of 1990; yellow-dog contract.

Labor-Management Reporting and Disclosure Act of 1959 (LMRDA) Administered by the National Labor Relations Board, LMRDA protects the rights of union members to organize, choose their own representatives, and bargain collectively. The Act also increased the power of the Department of Labor to investigate internal union financial and political affairs, and it strengthened prohibitions on secondary boycotts and placed restrictions on picketing to force recognition by nonunion companies. The law contains a union member's "bill of rights," sets forth ground rules for union elections, regulates the kind of person eligible for service as a union officer, and expands the list of unlawful employer actions. Also known as the *Landrum-Griffin Act.*

layoff **1.** Temporary termination of employees due to economic downturn, restructuring or downsizing, assembly line malfunction, equipment outage or replacement, or facility rehabilitation. Employees usually have recall rights to their jobs for a period of time, typically one year. **2.** The final step in a progressive disciplinary system, termination or firing for cause.

learning center A resource facility that offers materials in a variety of formats for individual study: audio- and videocassettes, computer-assisted and computer-managed instruction, interactive video, compact laser discs, 8mm and 16mm film, programmed and conventional books and workbooks, periodicals, manuals, organization documents, and a large number of programmed materials in audiovisual forms (sound-filmstrip, 35mm slides, overhead projections, and so on).

learning disabilities Problems with acquiring knowledge and skills, ranging from dyslexia, a serious learning problem where the printed page may seem like a scrambled maze of letters, to less severe disorders that can obstruct, encumber, or hamper learning success. Examples of the latter include simple memory deficiencies (inability to recall facts or steps in a process) and perceptual disorders (such as inability to judge time or distances, make comparisons, or anticipate obstacles or outcomes).

learningware Computer software programs designed to teach trainees specific knowledge and skills, such as troubleshooting, rather than to perform operations, such as preparing spreadsheets. *See also* courseware.

life cycle pension plan An actuarial-based pension concept developed by Robert D. Paul, vice chairman of the Martin E. Segal Company. Participants accrue a benefit which, on a lump sum basis, equals 10 percent of final five–year average pay. The plan is readily communicated to employees because it defines benefits in terms of a *multiple* rather than as a *percentage* of pay. The plan has been acclaimed by some as the **defined benefit plan** of choice for employers seeking to attract and retain fast-track employees and meet the needs of the next generation of employees. *See also* account balance pension; cash balance pension plan.

Lincoln incentive system An incentive plan in which employees work under a **guaranteed piecework plan** and, based on their performance (or merit rating), are given a share of the company's annual profits (less taxes, stockholders' dividends, and reserves for reinvestment). *See also* cash plan.

living benefits Plans that pay up to 30 percent of a life insurance death benefit either in a lump sum or in staggered payments to cover catastrophic or terminal illnesses ranging from cancer and bypass surgery to paying for nursing-home stays. Also called *accelerated death benefits*. *See also* viatical settlement.

living benefits rider (LBR) A clause added to insurance policies (usually whole or universal life policies) that provides payouts to the insured, ranging from 10 to 50 percent (average is 25 percent) of the face value of the policy following diagnosis of a grave or terminal medical condition, such as stroke, heart attack, coronary artery disease, kidney failure, or liver disease. Also called *accelerated benefit rider*.

lockout/tagout rule An **Occupational Safety and Health Act of 1970** rule that became effective October 31, 1989. The rule covers servicing and maintenance of machines and equipment in which an unexpected start-up or release of stored energy could injure employees. Employers must ensure that energy sources for equipment are turned off or disconnected and that the switch is locked or labeled with a warning tag. In addition they must develop an energy control system, ensure that new or repaired equipment can be locked, make use of additional safeguards when tags rather than locks are used, identify and implement specific procedures for the control of hazardous energy and for release of lockout/tagout, obtain standardized locks and tags, conduct annual inspections of energy control procedures, and train employees in specific energy control procedures.

long-term care (LTC) Long-term custodial care provided for the aged and infirm, the chronically ill or functionally disabled, victims of catastrophic illnesses such as stroke and heart attacks, and those with terminal illnesses. Care is provided in either home, medical facility, nursing home, or hospice, for active and retired employees, their spouses or other eligible dependents, or surviving spouses, and sometimes parents-in-law, who are severely and chronically impaired in performing the activities of daily living (such as eating, bathing, dressing, toileting, transportation, or getting around inside homes or doing other chores). *See also* family care program.

lump-sum distribution (LSD) or payment Payment of the total pension account to employees or their beneficiaries when they retire, change jobs, or become disabled, when a company terminates its retirement plan, or when an employee dies, leaving his or her spouse as beneficiary of a retirement plan. Under IRS rules, steps must be taken to defer taxes within 60 days of receipt of the lump sum or the money will be considered funds paid to the recipient and may be included in taxable income for the year. Such distributions may also be subject to an additional 10 percent penalty tax if the recipient has not reached age 59½ during the year in which the distribution was made or if the distribution was not made because of death or disability. A 1992 law requires retirement plan sponsors to begin withholding federal income taxes (20 percent) on certain LSDs in 1993 unless the funds are transferred directly to an **individual retirement account** or other qualified plan. It also simplifies access to the **rollover** option by removing virtually all restrictions on employees' right to roll over amounts received from a qualified retirement plan (previously, partial rollovers were restricted, and an employer's receipt of a partial rollover could threaten the plans qualification status).

M

MBTI	Myers-Briggs Type Indicator.
MC	Managed care.
MCCRA	Medicare Catastrophic Coverage Repeal Act of 1989.
MCO	Medicare carve-out.
MEWA	Multiple-employer welfare association.
MOSCA	McNamara-O'Hara Service Contract Act of 1965.
MPPAA	Multiemployer Pension Plan Amendments Act of 1980.
MPPP	Money-purchase pension plan.
MRAL	Mandatory Retirement Age Law of 1978.
MSA	Medical service agency.
MSAWA	Migrant and Seasonal Agricultural Worker Act of 1983.

mainstreaming The practice of keeping special needs trainees, those with mental, developmental, learning, emotional, or physical disabilities, in regular training classes rather than segregating them for separate instruction. Also called *inclusion*.

maintenance of benefits A health care cost-reduction plan in which employee benefits are paid by the secondary carrier only up to the amount the employer's plan would pay *less* any amount paid by the primary carrier. *See also* coordination of benefits; Medicare carve-out.

maintenance of membership A union-management agreement in which employees are not required to join the union, but union members employed by the firm must maintain their membership in the union for the duration of the contract. *See also* closed shop; open shop; union shop.

major life activities As defined by the **Americans with Disabilities Act of 1990,** they "include such things as caring for one's self, performing manual tasks, walking, seeing, hearing, speaking, breathing, learning, and working."

major medical coverage Supplementary insurance coverage (in addition

95

to basic coverage) that provides protection against large-scale surgical, hospital, or other medical expenses, treatment, and services. Typically, benefits are paid when a specific deductible has been met and are usually subject to coinsurance provisions.

managed care (MC) A monitoring system for health care benefits plans designed by the employer (not health care providers) to eliminate overuse by employing a staff of medical and nursing specialists to compare proposed medical care with accepted standards and provide reports to management. Managed care is a means of containing the costs of health care benefits plans, usually involving peer and utilization review, to eliminate overuse, unnecessary or inappropriate treatment, and fraud. In the broad sense, it includes everything from hospital review programs and case management to **health maintenance organizations** and **preferred provider organizations**.

managed chiro Managed chiropractic care, a relatively inexpensive component of employee benefits plans that is becoming increasingly popular. Sometimes involves establishing a network of practitioners, screening by a medical director, integrating chiropractic services with traditional medical services, forging lines of communication between chiropractors and physicians, and instituting quality assurance procedures, such as medical review, peer review inspections, patient surveys, and performance tracking.

managed competition plan A proposed form of health insurance plan under which health care providers bid for the job of providing care while state governments obtain coverage for the unemployed and part-time workers. Employers would be allowed to offer their own basic health policies or buy coverage through a nonprofit purchasing organization **(health insurance purchasing cooperatives)** set up by a state government board. In each state, the board would negotiate the best rates from HMO-type managed care networks that compete for consumers in a given geographic area. Under some plans, workers would pay taxes on part of the money employers now spend to provide health care benefits, that is; anything in excess of the cost of buying the least expensive basic health plan, such as membership in a **health maintenance organization.** Or employers might lose their tax deductions on what they pay. Or both. The idea is to get health care businesses to cut prices to attract customers—to compete to provide customers with more for their money. *See also* play or pay model; single-payer plan; universal health care plan.

managed pharmacy network A consortium consisting of one or more carefully selected chain pharmacy organizations in a particular region supplemented by independent pharmacies, established to provide better geographic access and meaningful discounts below retail pricing for employers. Pricing typically uses the formula of Average Wholesale Price plus a $2 dispensing fee. In addition to offering prices that are 15 to 20 percent lower than card systems, managed pharmacy systems take advantage of point-of-sale technology, which allows participating pharmacies to verify coverage before the prescription is dispensed.

management development Programs designed to meet the needs of an organization for successors to current managers, to help current managers to become more effective, and to provide additional managers to meet the need for expansion of the industry or organization. The programs focus on the management of environmental factors, work force, employee attitudes and values, and technological change. They develop knowledge and skills in leadership and group dynamics, strategic planning and goal setting, organization theory and applications, leadership styles, motivation theory and applications, coaching and team building, and managing change and innovation. Strategies include formal training and education, seminars and workshops, discussion groups and team building, role playing and case studies, simulations, independent study, guided self-analysis and assessment, and coaching.

mandatory assignment A state law that establishes a barrier to **managed care** (eight states currently have such a law). The law prevents insurers from contractually requiring providers to accept the plan's payment as payment in full, except for applicable deductibles and **coinsurance**. *See also* fair reimbursement law.

mandatory bargaining item In labor-management contract negotiations, an item that must be considered and negotiated if it is introduced by either party; for example, pay and benefits. *See also* voluntary bargaining item.

Mandatory Retirement Age Law of 1978 (MRAL) An Act that prohibits forced retirement of any employee under 70 years of age. Exempt are employees whose jobs have bona fide occupational qualifications, college professors, and business executives. *See also* bona fide occupational qualification.

Manhart Decision A 1978 Supreme Court Decision that the use of sex-based mortality tables for determining employee contributions to retirement plans violates **Title VII** of the **Civil Rights Act of 1964** (sex discrimination). *See also* Norris Decision.

market pricing Setting salaries or salary ranges by functional areas or job families on the basis of salary surveys or market pressures with little or no regard for internal ranking or equity. Typically used where there are severe shortages in certain skills areas.

market value plan A type of executive incentive plan that permits executives to purchase company stock, usually with funds borrowed from the company at low interest. The borrowed funds are either repaid or amortized by means of credits representing compensation for services or bonuses based on performance. *See also* bonus payment; book value plan; self-designed pay plan; stock options.

massive layoff Defined by the **Worker Adjustment and Retraining Notification Act of 1988** as a reduction in force that is not the result of a plant closing and results in an employment loss at a single site during any thirty-day period for at least 33 percent of the employees and at least 50 employees.

maximum payment period The lifetime maximum number of days for which a health care insurance policy will pay for confinement in a health care facility or **alternate long-term care facility**, including any rider benefits. *See also* daily maximum.

McNamara-O'Hara Service Contract Act of 1965 (MOSCA) Requires federal contractors who provide services to the federal government at a cost in excess of $2,500 to pay minimum (prevailing) wage rates and provide prevailing fringe benefits, including medical or hospital care, unemployment benefits, life insurance, disability and sickness insurance, accident insurance, vacation and holiday pay, costs of apprenticeship or similar programs, and other bona fide fringe benefits. *See also* Davis-Bacon Acts of 1931 and 1964; prevailing wage rate.

med-arb An **alternative dispute resolution procedure** in which a neutral party is selected to serve as both mediator and arbitrator. Med-arb combines the voluntary strategies of persuasion and discussion, as in mediation, with an arbitrator's authority to issue a final and binding decision. *See also* arbitration; expedited arbitration; fact-finding; mediation; mini-trial; rent-a-judge; summary jury trial.

mediation A form of negotiation used to resolve individual and group disputes, including labor-management disagreements. Mediation is confidential and private and always involves a neutral third party whose job is to help the individuals or groups reach a voluntary settlement of the issue. Mediators have no power to make decisions or judgments or to enforce an agreement. Their role is that of facilitator and expediter. *See also* alternative dispute resolution procedure; arbitration; med-arb; mini-trial; negotiation; rent-a-judge; summary jury trial.

Medicaid Medical benefits, including hospitalization, payment of health care providers, prescription drugs, and the like, provided for the low income, the poor, and the indigent without charge (no premiums and no deductibles). Eligibility is determined by three tests:

(1) age 65 or older, blind, or physically or mentally disabled; (2) monthly income not in excess of the maximum allowable amount set by the state; and (3) total assets lower than the established limits. The federal government reimburses states for a substantial portion of Medicaid benefits paid so long as the state's Medicaid program falls within prescribed federal guidelines. In general, coverage is limited to Aid to Families with Dependent Children and **Supplemental Security Income**, low-income pregnant women, low-income children under the age of five, and low-income persons in institutions and nursing homes. *See also* Medicare; Medicare Catastrophic Coverage Act of 1988.

medically necessary In health care benefits, a requirement for payment of medical and surgical charges. A service or supply is usually considered medically necessary when it is offered by a physician, is effective in treating the condition for which it is prescribed, is part of a course of treatment generally accepted by the American medical community, does not duplicate other services or supplies used to treat the condition, is not experimental, and is intended to restore health and extend life.

medical screening Preemployment medical examinations used primarily to make the best use of employees by placing them in suitable positions. Also used to reduce absenteeism and turnover, avoid **workers' compensation** and other claims against the organization, make needed adjustments to the work area to accommodate the employee, safeguard the health and safety of the employee, other employees, clients, and customers, and identify substance abusers before they are hired. *See also* medical underwriting.

medical self-care Programs that encourage employees to become better consumers and self-healers to achieve savings on medical plans. Instead of relying on specialized medical care, employees are encouraged to attend seminars and use books, pamphlets, and other materials dealing with preventing and treating common health problems, get more involved in treatment decisions, and work with their physicians to improve the quality and reduce the costs of their health care.

medical service agency (MSA) A coalition of **managed care** organizations designed to overcome the problems of medical service costs and cost-shifting through increased copayments, higher deductibles, balance billing practices, and so on.

medical underwriting The use of physical examinations and tests of body fluids (urine and blood) by insurers to screen out high-risk applicants for life or health insurance (such as those carrying HIV, the AIDS virus). *See also* medical screening.

Medicare A federal health insurance program for people 65 or older and certain disabled people under 65 designed to cover medical needs. Medicare is operated by the Health Care Financing Administration of the U.S. Department of Health and Human Services. Unlike **Medicaid**, it is not a financially need-based program; it provides benefits regardless of the financial status of the recipient. It consists of two parts: Part A, hospital insurance, which helps pay for inpatient hospital care, some inpatient care in a skilled nursing facility, and hospice care; and Part B, medical insurance, which helps pay for medically necessary physician's services, outpatient hospital services, home health care, and a number of other medical services and supplies that are not covered by the hospital insurance part of Medicare. Part A is financed by part of the payroll (FICA) tax that also pays for Social Security. Part B is financed by monthly premiums paid by people who choose to enroll. *See also* Federal Insurance Contributions Act of 1935; Medicaid; Medicare Catastrophic Coverage Act of 1988.

Medicare carve-out (MCO) A health care cost-cutting strategy in which employee benefits are adjusted according to Medicare payout; if Medicare pays more, no additional benefit is paid; if Medicare pays less, a supplement is paid. *See also* coordination of benefits; maintenance of benefits.

Medicare Catastrophic Coverage Act of 1988 (CATCAP) A law that improved some Medicare benefits but imposed supplemental and graduated premiums on people 65 and older who had income tax liability. Congress repealed the CATCAP surtax November 22, 1989 (retroactive to January 1, 1989). All that remains of the catastrophic coverage is protection against spousal impoverishment (protection of the at-home spouse when the other spouse enters a nursing home and applies for Medicaid), a Medicare buy-in for the impoverished (payment of Medicare Part B premiums), and new Medicaid provisions for pregnant mothers and infants. *See also* Medicaid; Medicare; Medicare Catastrophic Coverage Repeal Act of 1989.

Medicare Catastrophic Coverage Repeal Act of 1989 (MCCRA) An act that preserved one of the features of the CATCAP law—protection against spousal impoverishment. It was enacted December 13, 1989, and provides some financial protection for the at-home or community spouse when the institutionalized spouse is in a nursing home. The law also sets minimums and maximums for the amount of assets a community (noninstitutionalized) spouse can retain. Excluded from the computation of assets is the value of the home, personal effects, and household goods. *See also* Medicare Catastrophic Coverage Act of 1988.

Medicare supplement insurance plans At the direction of Congress, the National Association of Insurance Commissioners (NAIC), with the help of consumer groups and industry representatives, developed a new set of standards for Medicare supplemental insurance plans. Under these guidelines, beginning July 30, 1992, insurance companies began to offer up to ten standardized NAIC plans, designated Plans A through J. Companies that sell Medicare supplement insurance must offer Plan A, the most basic plan, and may offer Plans B through J depending on market conditions. In forty-four states and the District of Columbia, insurance companies are now allowed to sell only the ten new standardized medigap policies. In three other states, Delaware, Pennsylvania, and Vermont, insurers now sell six of the ten. Three states (Massachusetts, Minnesota, and Wisconsin) have created a standard plan plus standard riders.

medigap insurance Private health insurance designed to supplement Medicare (or company insurance) by bridging the gap between the approved rate and the deductible and the provider's charge. Therefore, it typically pays some, but not all, of the medical bills that Medicare (or the company's carrier) doesn't pay. Part B, Medicare, pays 80 percent of the "allowed" amount. The remainder is paid by supplemental (medigap) insurance, Medicaid, or the patient.

mentoring The practice of having senior, experienced, and respected managers or staffers serve as role models, coaches, counselors, advisors, and advocates for younger or less experienced persons.

merit pay Increased compensation paid for outstanding performance of assigned duties and tasks. The approach assumes, or at least implies, that an objective performance appraisal system is in effect which adequately determines the performance of individual employees. If such a system does not exist, merit pay should not be used. And it should never be linked with economic conditions or increases in the cost of living. *See also* merit rating.

merit rating A systematic and orderly means of appraising and rating performance; ratings used as a basis for incentive plans such as pay-for-performance. *See also* incentive plan; merit pay.

method A basic approach to instruction. Instruction methods include conventional lecture, conference, demonstration, and performance as well as tutorials, case studies, and simulation, or a combination of the foregoing. *See also* instructional strategy.

Migrant and Seasonal Agricultural Worker Act of 1983 (MSAWA) An act designed to protect migrant and seasonal agricultural workers from unfair labor practices, unhealthful or unsafe living, housing, and working conditions, or discrimination because they have, with just cause, filed a complaint, initiated a proceeding, or testified in any such proceedings relating to the provisions of the Act. It requires employers to obtain a certificate of registration as a farm labor contractor. They are also required to disclose in writing to each worker the place of employment, the wage rates to be paid, the crops and kinds of activities in which the worker may be employed, the period of employment, the transportation, housing, and any other benefit to be provided and their costs, if any, the existence of any strike or other work stoppage, slowdown, or interruption of operations by employees, and any arrangements for commissions or other benefits accruing to the contractor or association resulting from sales to the workers.

minimum wage law A minimum wage level established by Congress as a part of the **Fair Labor Standards Act**. The minimum wage was increased from $3.80 to $4.25 per hour in April 1991 (businesses grossing less than $500,000 thousand annually are specifically exempted). The same legislation established a training wage (subminimum) for teenagers entering the work force, which started at $3.35 per hour and rose to $3.61 per hour in April 1991. The training wage (restricted to 25 percent of an organization's total work force) applied to workers aged 16 to 19 and could last no longer than ninety days. The training wage expired in March 1993. States may have minimums that are higher than those mandated by the federal government.

mini-trial An **alternative dispute resolution procedure** involving confidential, nonbinding exchange of information with the objective of achieving a prompt and cost-effective settlement of complex litigation. The process seeks to narrow areas of disagreement, reconcile collateral issues, and encourage a fair and equitable settlement. *See also* arbitration; fact-finding; med-arb; mediation; rent-a-judge; summary jury trial.

mommy track A term triggered by Felice Schwartz ("Management Women and the New Facts of Life," *Harvard Business Review*, January–February 1989). She commented on the need for corporate flexibility to accommodate two types of women who need quite different career paths: the Career and Family Woman (women who opt for motherhood regardless of the consequences for career development and progression—the mommy track) and the Career Primary Woman (women who are willing to make the most of every opportunity for professional development even if it means sacrifices in their personal lives). *See also* daddy track; grandpa track.

money-purchase pension plan (MPPP) A type of defined contribution pension plan in which the employer contribution is mandatory and is usually based on a fixed percentage of annual compensation.

MPPPs are established and maintained to provide for payment of determinable benefits to employees over a period of years, usually for life, following retirement. *See also* profit-sharing plan; Section 401(k), Internal Revenue Code.

moonlighting The practice of holding a second full-time or part-time job in addition to one's normal, full-time occupation. Moonlighting has been prohibited in many organizations because management believes that it detracts from performance of the primary job due to either physical or emotional exhaustion or both.

multicorporate health care Consortiums of organizations organized to provide health care to their employees by contracting with health care management firms consisting of physicians, registered nurses and nurse practitioners, therapists, data and information specialists, and support staff. Such cooperative arrangements yield economies of scale.

multiemployer benefits plan An employee benefits plan to which more than one employer is required to contribute and which is maintained in accordance with the provisions of one or more collective bargaining agreements. The **Employee Retirement Income Security Act of 1974** defined the original rules for such plans; the **Multiemployer Pension Plan Amendments Act of 1980** increased the number of rules.

Multiemployer Pension Plan Amendments Act of 1980 (MPPAA) Legislation that completely revised Title IV of the **Employee Retirement Income Security Act of 1974** as it applies to multiemployer pension plans. Although too numerous to describe here, the additions included rules relating to administration, reporting, fiduciary responsibility, and enforcement, and for pension plans, to participation, vesting, funding, and termination insurance. *See also* multiemployer benefits plan.

multiple-employer welfare association (MEWA) A cooperative established to enable members, mainly small employers, to purchase health care coverage at lower costs.

Myers-Briggs Type Indicator (MBTI) A popular psychological test, refined over a period of four years, used primarily but not exclusively in the corporate world by trainers and organization development specialists in team building and communications training. The MBTI divides people into sixteen distinguishable personality types. Although highly popular, the test also has its critics, who see it as encouraging managers to view personality tests as the easy answer to organization problems.

N

NHCE   Non-highly-compensated employee.
NLRA   National Labor Relations Acts of 1935 and 1947.
NMMHMO   Network and mixed model health maintenance organi-
              zation.
NQSO   Nonqualified stock options.

National Labor Relations Act of 1935 (NLRA) An act increasing government power to ensure employee collective bargaining rights and
prohibiting management from engaging in the following unfair labor practices: (1) interfering with, restraining, or coercing employees in the exercise of their right to join, or assist in the organization
of, a union or to refrain from doing so; (2) dominating or interfering
with the formation or administration of a labor organization, or contributing financially or otherwise supporting it; (3) discriminating in
hiring or tenure of employment or imposing any term or condition
of employment to encourage or discourage membership in any labor organization; (4) discharging or otherwise discriminating
against employees because they have given testimony under the
Act; and (5) refusing to bargain collectively with representatives of
its employees. The Act also created the National Labor Relations
Board to supervise and certify representation elections and prevent
unfair labor practices. It also authorized the Board to appoint a representative in court cases involving unions to investigate, prosecute,
and judge. Amended by the **Labor-Management Relations Act of
1947** (Taft-Hartley), the **Labor-Management Reporting and Disclosure Act of 1959** (Landrum-Griffin), and the Labor Management Cooperation Act of 1978. Also known as the *Wagner Act*. *See also* National Labor Relations Act of 1947.
National Labor Relations Act of 1947 (NLRA) An act administered by
the National Labor Relations Board and general counsel. The legislation made it the responsibility of the President, subject to Senate

confirmation, to appoint a general counsel to a four-year term to serve as investigator and prosecutor in court cases involving unions, thereby protecting the general counsel's autonomy. The Act applies to virtually all industries involved in interstate commerce with a few exceptions. *See also* National Labor Relations Act of 1935.

needs assessment A means of determining the training and development programs needed by the organization, employee groups, or individual employees to make the organization competitive in its industry, improve productivity, build employee morale and job satisfaction, and improve promotion potential and foster career development. Needs assessment identifies gaps in capabilities, abilities, and on-the-job results (performance) and places the identified needs in priority order for resolution. *See also* front-end analysis.

negligent hiring 1. A legal tort recognized by more than 20 states. Negligent hiring may be charged when an employer fails to exercise care and caution in hiring and fails to note the consequences of hiring an unsuitable person for a position. Under some conditions, such as contacts with large groups of people and access to private property, this means that the employer is expected to conduct an inquiry into an applicant's background, short of an independent investigation into an applicant's criminal record. *See also respondeat superior.* 2. Employment policies or procedures that omit or neglect to do things that a reasonable person, guided by ordinary considerations as well as the law, would do, or doing something that a reasonable and prudent person would not do. Therefore, employers have the right and the duty to carefully investigate a potential employee's work-related background and in doing so they are generally protected by the law. *See also* negligent job references; restatement of tort.

negligent job references Failure to exercise due care in providing information about current or past employees when references are requested by other organizations or agencies. *See also* negligent hiring; *respondeat superior.*

negotiation In labor-management relations, a process for reaching agreement between or among two or more individuals or groups who have conflicting interests, acting either for themselves or as representatives of organizations. Negotiation may take the form of arbitration or mediation. *See also* arbitration; mediation.

network and mixed model health maintenance organization (NMMHMO) A combination of the following types of health maintenance organizations: group practice health maintenance organization, independent practice association, and staff model health maintenance organization. *See also* health maintenance organization.

networking The process of acquiring, cultivating, and using a community of professionals to get advice, information, assistance, contacts, and referrals. It is a means of expanding one's learning resources at little or no cost.

no frills health plan A new type of low-cost health policy made available to small businesses (typically fewer than 50 workers) by laws enacted by the state legislatures of Florida, Illinois, Kansas, Kentucky, Maryland, Missouri, North Dakota, Rhode Island, Virginia, and Washington. The new policies cost less because the law exempts insurers from covering several kinds of care mandated by the states in most health plans. Examples are care by a chiropractor or podiatrist, drug abuse treatment, and mental health costs. The plans are designed to help businesses kept out of the market by high and rising costs of health care insurance premiums. Similar legislation has been introduced in Congress.

noncompete agreement A contract in which an employee agrees not to compete with an employer during employment or for a specified time following termination of employment. Such an agreement may restrict the employees from working for direct competitors when they leave. Noncompete agreements are not controlled by federal law, but in some states laws limit the way in which the agreement can be used by employers. Also known as a *restrictive covenant*.

noncontributory benefits plan A plan in which the employer pays the entire cost or full premiums of a funding plan for paying employee benefits.

nondirective counseling An approach to counseling characterized by actions aimed at establishing and maintaining the conditions necessary for the counselee to achieve insight into his or her problem and thereby achieve control over it. Nondirective counselors do not diagnose, interpret, advise, suggest, reason, persuade, probe, or pass judgment. Rather, they demonstrate warmth and acceptance and concentrate on reflecting and clarifying attitudes. *See also* directive counseling.

nonexempt employee A worker covered by (not exempted from) the overtime pay provisions of the **Fair Labor Standards Act of 1938**. Nonexempt employees include hourly paid employees (most occupations related to production, maintenance, and services functions where pay is directly related to the number of hours worked) and some nonexempt salaried workers (clerical, administrative, and paraprofessional job categories).

non-highly-compensated employee (NHCE) An employee who owns less than 5 percent or who is not a family member of owners, who earns less than $75,000 from an employer or earns less than $50,000 from the employer and is in the bottom 80 percent of employees, or any officer earning less than $45,000. *See also* highly compensated employee.

nonqualified pension plan A plan that does not meet IRS rules and requirements, such as those that provide benefits in excess of those allowed, and therefore does not qualify for favorable tax treatment.

nonqualified stock options (NQSO) A form of stock option plan that does not meet all of the requirements of Section 422A of the Internal Revenue Code for incentive options. Nonqualified options usually have a ten–year option term and are usually priced at 100 percent of market value at the time of the grant.

Norris Decision A 1983 Supreme Court decision stating that an annuity option in a retirement plan that paid smaller monthly benefits to women than to men discriminated on the basis of sex and was a violation of **Title VII** of the **Civil Rights Act of 1964.** *See also* Manhart Decision.

notice A legal doctrine that applies in wrongful discharge cases. In effect it asks, "Did the employer give the employee forewarning of the possible consequences of the employee's disciplinary conduct?"

nursing home coverage An insurance policy that pays a certain amount per day for services provided in a skilled nursing facility or a smaller amount per day for services in an alternate long-term care facility. Typically specifies a benefit limit stated in terms of the combined number of days for which the subscriber will be paid. Also usually includes an elimination period, the number of consecutive days of confinement needed to qualify for benefits.

O

OAA	Older Americans Acts of 1965, 1978, and 1992.
OASDHI	Old Age, Survivors, Disability, and Health Insurance Program.
OBRA	Omnibus Budget Reconciliation Acts of 1987, 1989, and 1990.
OD	Organization development.
OEHMO	Open-ended health maintenance organization.
OEP	Open-ended plan.
OJT	On-the-job training.
OSHA	Occupational Safety and Health Act of 1970.
OT	Organizational transformation.
OWBPA	Older Workers Benefit Protection Act of 1990.
125	*See* Section 125, Internal Revenue Code.
127	*See* Section 127, Internal Revenue Code.

occupational disability Inability to perform one's usual occupation or work for pay due to accident or injury. Usually entitles the person to workers' compensation or similar benefits. *See also* disability; occupational disease.

occupational disease A disease which arises out of and in the course of employment and for which a person is entitled to benefits under workers' compensation or similar law. *See also* occupational disability; occupational illness; occupational injury.

occupational field The largest meaningful configuration of human work performance. An occupational field consists of all logically related or skills-related jobs. For example, the health services occupational field includes such jobs as physician, registered nurse, licensed practical nurse, and a host of other specialties and subspecialties.

occupational illness An abnormal condition or disorder caused by exposure to environmental factors associated with employment, including acute and chronic illnesses that may be caused by absorption, inhalation, ingestion, or direct contact with toxic substances or harmful agents. *See also* occupational disease; occupational injury; Occupational Safety and Health Act of 1970.

occupational injury Injury sustained on the job that results in medical treatment other than first aid, loss of consciousness, restriction of work, loss of one or more workdays, restriction of motion, or transfer to another job. *See also* occupational disease; occupational illness; Occupational Safety and Health Act of 1970.

Occupational Safety and Health Act of 1970 (OSHA) Requires employers to provide safe and healthful working conditions, protection against hazards that might cause illness, injury, or death, including hazardous work conditions, methods, materials, and substances. Under OSHA, every employer must be familiar with mandatory OSHA standards and make copies available for employees to review, inform employees about OSHA, inspect workplace conditions to ensure that they conform to safety and health standards, remove or guard hazards, and report and keep records of injuries and occupational illnesses (firms with 11 or more employees). The Act applies to all employers engaged in interstate commerce and is enforced by the Department of Labor. Also known as the *Williams-Steiger Act*. *See also* occupational illness; occupational injury.

off-label drug A drug prescribed by a physician for use for a condition not approved by the Food and Drug Administration for that particular condition (although it may be approved by the FDA for a different condition).

offset pension formula A formula that results in the subtraction of a portion (limited by IRS regulations) of an individual's Social Security annuity from a defined amount to determine the benefit from the pension plan.

Old Age, Survivors, Disability, and Health Insurance Program (OAS-DHI) A successor of the **Social Security Act of 1935**. An omnibus social bill passed by the Congress that covers retirement, survivors, and disability insurance (Social Security), hospital and medical insurance for the aged and disabled (Medicare and Medicaid), black-lung benefits for miners, Supplemental Security Income, unemployment insurance, and public assistance in welfare systems.

Older Americans Act of 1965 (OAA) An act to assist older people to secure equal opportunity to the full and free enjoyment of an adequate income in retirement, the best possible physical and mental health, and opportunity for employment without discrimination because of age, among other objectives. Congress has reaffirmed its support for OAA programs 12 times through amendments and reauthorization actions. *See* Older Americans Act Amendments of 1992.

Older Americans Act Amendments of 1992 Amends the **Older Americans Act of 1965** by including support to family members and other persons providing voluntary care to older persons and needing long-term care services. Provides training and employment counseling to older Americans who have poor employment prospects and economic need. Signed into law by President Bush on September 30, 1992.

Older Workers Benefit Protection Act of 1990 (OWBPA) An Act signed into law by President Bush on October 16, 1990. It requires that early retirement incentive plans be "consistent with the *relevant* purpose or purposes of this act." It also makes it clear that the **Age Discrimination in Employment Act of 1967** has authority over employee benefits. Although ADEA requires employers to provide equal benefits to all workers, it allows reductions in benefits for older workers in cases where added employer costs are incurred as a result of providing those benefits to older workers. The Older Workers Benefit Protection Act of 1990 restores the ADEA to what it was prior to Supreme Court decisions eliminating the requirement for employers to justify lower benefits for older workers by showing increased costs or other economic considerations. Under the law, all waivers and releases of age discrimination must be voluntary. Specifically, all waivers of ADEA rights must (1) be part of an understandable and written agreement between the employer and the employee; (2) refer to rights or claims arising under ADEA; (3) be exclusive of rights or claims that may arise after the date the waiver is signed; (4) be in exchange for consideration in addition to anything of value to which the employee is already entitled; (5) include a written notice to the employee to consult with an attorney before signing the agreement; (6) allow employees at least 21 days to consider the agreement (or 45 days if part of employment termination); and (7) include a provision that permits the employee to revoke the agreement within seven days.

Omnibus Budget Reconciliation Act of 1987 (OBRA) Made significant changes to funding and termination insurance rules applicable to defined benefit pension plans as well as changes that affect defined contribution plans. The Act modified rules that limit the holding of employer securities by employee benefits plans and restricts the availability of an estate tax deduction for sales of employer securities to an employee stock option (ownership) plan.

Omnibus Budget Reconciliation Act of 1989 (OBRA) Modified several of the continuation of health care coverage requirements of the **Con-**

solidated Omnibus Budget Reconciliation Act of 1986. Part of this bill relates to Medicare as a secondary payor and specifically to periods of coverage for qualified beneficiaries other than the covered employee, which "shall not terminate before the close of the 36-month period beginning on the date the covered employee becomes entitled to [Medicare] benefits under title XVIII of the Social Security Act" (36 months after the date of the original qualifying event). Another part of the bill relates to the extension of the **Employee Educational Assistance Act of 1978.**

Omnibus Budget Reconciliation Act of 1990 (OBRA) The first federal child care legislation passed since World War II. The Act provides for a three-year, $2.5 billion block grant for states to distribute to parents and day care providers. Recipients of grants can spend them as they wish, but they must meet minimum state health and safety standards. The Act also lays the groundwork for a broad federal policy to encourage as well as regulate those who provide child care services. OBRA 1990 also increases Medicare Part B premiums incrementally from $29.90 as of January 1, 1991, to $46.10 as of 1995. It increases the annual Medicare Part B deductible from $75 to $100 annually, and extends the 1.45 percent Medicare tax from its current cap of $51,300 per year to $125,000. OBRA 1990 also mandates that states expand Medicaid coverage to poor children up to the age of 18 by the year 2000; requires Medicaid to pay Medicare's Part B premiums, coinsurance, and deductibles for people at the poverty line; gives states more flexibility to provide home- and community-based long-term care services under Medicaid; and requires pharmaceutical companies to offer state programs with discounts on prescriptions. The Act prohibits both the sale of duplicative policies to Medicare beneficiaries and the sale of any medigap insurance to low-income older Americans who already receive additional health coverage from the Medicaid program. *See also* Deficit Reduction Act of 1984.

on-call time Off-duty hours during which an employee is required to remain on call either at the work premises or so close to it that he or she cannot effectively use the time for personal purposes. According to the Fair Labor Standards Act as amended, such restrictive on-call time is compensable as working time. An employee who is required to leave word where he or she can be reached is not considered to be on working time, nor is one who wears a beeper while off duty.

on-site or near-site child care center A child care facility for company employees either owned and operated by the employer, constructed by the employer and donated to nonprofit employee-operated groups, or contracted by the employer with a for-profit or not-for-profit organization.

on-the-job training (OJT) Planned and organized training conducted at the workplace, in the office, shop, laboratory, or in the field, on the production line, on the construction site, or behind the counter by a co-worker or supervisor. It is provided by means of demonstration and example, guided practice, and feedback on performance.

open-ended health maintenance organization (OEHMO) A form of managed care plan designed to contain health care costs by limiting employee choices through the use of such techniques as preauthorization of hospital admission and utilization review. They are "point-of-service" HMOs where there is a primary care physician, and utilization of medical services is tightly managed. *See also* health maintenance organization; preferred provider organization.

open-ended plan (OEP) A plan offered by health maintenance organizations that allows members to seek health care from nonparticipating physicians and other health care professionals. In exchange for using these providers, members pay higher premiums, deductibles, and copayments. Also called *open-ended option.*

open enrollment 1. A system where enrollment in company training programs is open to any employee upon application and approval by his or her immediate supervisor. Enrollment forms and schedules are mailed to branches and offices with deadlines for applying. **2.** A period of time during which individuals may sign up for medical or health insurance, for example, people who failed to sign up for Medicare's Medical Insurance (Part B) when they first became eligible, normally at age 65, or who dropped Part B for some valid reason.

open pay system A pay system in which employees know what other workers in the organization are being paid; for example, the U.S. government general schedule is openly published. *See also* closed pay system; pay secrecy.

open shop A nonunionized organization in which workers decide for themselves whether they join the union. *See also* agency shop; closed shop; maintenance of membership; union shop.

Operation Transition A massive outplacement program launched by the Department of Defense (DOD) in 1991. The effort is designed to help companies tap the new source of labor that will be created by plans to cut the Department of Defense military and civilian work force over the next 5 to 7 years. Features of the system: on-line access to an automated database of occupations organized by geographic location via a 900 phone number, an electronic bulletin board allowing employers to place free ads for specific jobs; DOD verification of candidate's training and experience at no charge; DOD payment of all moving and storage costs for up to one year for successful candidates for positions; and additional training paid for by DOD for outplaced personnel even if hired by private sector employers.

organizational survey Periodic and systematic examination and analysis of the organizational structure to ensure that it is consistent with current operating requirements. Such surveys consist of seven steps: planning, data collection, interpretation of data, development of solutions, presenting recommendations, installing and following up recommendations, and evaluating results.

organizational transformation (OT) A general term covering new or cutting-edge training programs designed to reshape or transform organizations by stimulating motivation, innovation, and excellence through teamwork, empowerment, and participation. OT is viewed as the final stage of a continuum consisting of management-employee development, organization development, and organization transformation. In essence, it is a long-range program to involve all employees in a major effort to change an organization's culture, values, and management processes and thereby improve productivity, product/service quality, results, and employee satisfaction. *See also* organization development.

organization climate survey A data collection instrument used to obtain diagnostic information about an organization and used to study its climate and culture. Topics include communication, creativity, pay and benefits, management practices, policies, product and service quality, supervisory practices, the job itself, work conditions, and so on. An organization climate survey gathers employee attitudes, beliefs, feelings, opinions and perceptions, not facts. Also known as *employee attitude survey; employee opinion survey; job satisfaction survey; organization characteristics survey; work climate survey.*

organization development (OD) A planned and systematic strategy for changing and improving the management and operation of an enterprise to increase effectiveness, enhance productivity, boost return on investment, improve the quality of work life, and raise the level of employee job satisfaction. In more specific terms, the purpose of the OD process is to clarify the mission, goals, and objectives of the organization; align and integrate individual employee, unit, and enterprise goals; make the organization more effective; deal effectively with technical, managerial, and human problems; improve cooperation, collaboration, communication, and teamwork between managers and their subordinates and among units; promote openness and free discussion of differences, issues, and problems; improve decision-making processes and promote employee and union acceptance of decisions; build acceptance of and ability to deal with change; improve individual and team performance and interpersonal relationships; and find and articulate consensus and translate it into action. *See also* human resources development; organizational transformation.

outcomes management Attributed to Paul M. Elwood, Jr., M.D., developer of the HMO concept twenty years ago, outcomes management is a system for measuring and analyzing the impact of ordinary medical care on the clinical status, function, and well-being of patients. The system relies on epidemiologic principles for making comparisons. "Outcomes" include better quality of life, how soon employees return to work, whether they have pain or resumed their normal activities, whether they feel better, and so on, as well as such traditional clinical measures as lowered blood sugar, blood pressure, and cholesterol level.

outpatient facility A facility designed to provide one-time or continuing health and medical services to individuals who have not been admitted to hospital inpatient care.

outplacement Job-finding counseling and assistance provided to displaced or terminated employees by the organization dismissing the employee. Services may include workshops and training, individual assessment and counseling, access to computerized databanks of job openings, resume preparation, separate on-site facilities (even private offices) for conducting job searches, secretarial assistance, and financial counseling. *See also* group outplacement.

outsourcing 1. The practice of hiring outside consultants, trainers, or other types of professionals or technicians rather than employing full-time personnel. It is a strategy for freeing management to concentrate on critical functions and activities by transferring routine and repetitive tasks to a third party. **2.** Using external consulting firms and service agencies to administer benefit plans, such as flexible benefit plans. *See also* insourcing.

overtime Work performed in excess of 40 hours in any week for which, under the **Fair Labor Standards Act of 1938,** employees must be paid one-and-one-half times their normal wage rates. Some organizations pay more than one-and-one-half times normal wage rates and some pay for hours worked in excess of 37.5 hours.

P

PA	Privacy Act of 1974.
PAR	Preadmission review.
PAT	Preadmission testing.
PAYSOP	Payroll-based stock option plan.
PBGC	Pension Benefit Guarantee Corporation.
PDA	Pregnancy Discrimination Act of 1978.
PDP	Prescription drug plan.
PEPP	Permanent-equity pension plan.
PFS	Pay for skills.
POS	Point-of-service.
PPA	1. Pension Protection Act of 1987. 2. Pension Portability Act of 1992.
PPO	Preferred provider organization.
PRO	Peer review organization.
PSP	Performance share plan.
PSS	Performance support system.
PT	Performance technology.
PTPA	Portal-to-Portal Act of 1947.
PUP	Performance unit plan.

paid time off 1. Vacation days (typically eleven days per year the first year of employment, increasing to twenty-four days after thirty years), sick days (typically ten days per year with carryover allowed by almost half of American companies), and **personal days** (provided by only 25 percent of American companies) away from the workplace paid for by the employer. **2.** A flexible benefit plan option in which employees are given the opportunity to buy and sell paid time off. They can buy additional vacation time by trading other benefits for it or sell it for benefits they prefer. *See also* flexible benefits/flex benefits program; pooling.

patient advocate A medical professional, usually a registered nurse with clinical experience and medical/surgical background, assigned by an employer or an insurance carrier to work with patients and their physicians and coordinate health care from preadmission to discharge.

pay adjustment An effect of inflation, restructuring, other changes in economic conditions, the competitive status of an organization, union demands, or the expectations of workers based on such traditional considerations as experience, seniority, increased responsibility, or simply job tenure. Pay adjustments take the form of raises and salary cuts. They may also be called *general increases* or *across-the-board adjustments*.

pay-as-you-go strategy A plan for meeting retiree medical liabilities in which benefits are funded as required. The company puts money back into the business instead of into a portfolio of securities.

payback agreement Essentially a contract between a company and relocated employees. Payback agreements state that, if the employee voluntarily leaves the company within a specified period of time (usually one or two years) from the effective date of his or her transfer and receipt of relocation benefits for any reason other than to accept other employment at the same company or one of its subsidiaries, the individual must repay the company, on a prorated basis, all relocation-related expenses, reimbursements, and tax allowances paid on the employee's behalf.

pay compression Describes the situation where the normal differences in pay between successive job levels or grades gradually erode or actually disappear due to inflation (new hires may receive equal or more pay than workers who have been in the organization for years).

pay for performance A compensation system in which employees share the risks of business with owners/investors. They earn more when productivity, sales, and profits rise and less when they decline. Such plans typically start with reduced base wages and salaries but bonuses are awarded when production targets, sales, or some other measure of performance is achieved.

pay for skills (PFS) A program designed to keep employee productivity, commitment, job satisfaction, and morale high and turnover down. Although there are several forms of the program, the most common approach is to define and document the specific skills and knowledge required for each job in the organization and communicate them to employees along with notification that if and when they have mastered the requirements for a particular job, they will be promoted to that position. *See also* behavior-based incentive compensation.

pay grades Pay classes, rates, or steps for different jobs of approximately equal difficulty, importance, or value as determined by job evaluation and used for pay purposes.

payroll-based stock option plan (PAYSOP) Formerly called TRASOP. Defined contribution plans, established under the Tax Reduction Act of 1975, used to transfer employer stock to employees to provide equity ownership to workers. Describes modifications to tax regulations under the Tax Reduction Act of 1975 and its amendments relating tax credits to distributions that are proportional to payroll. *See also* employee stock option (ownership) plan.

pay secrecy An issue of considerable importance in many organizations. Pay secrecy concerns whether or not employees should know what other workers in their organization are being paid. *See also* closed pay system; open pay system.

pay steps Specified levels within a pay grade. Employees progress from step to step on the basis of such factors as time in grade, performance, educational level, or acquisition of new job skills.

pay structure A tabular or graphic representation of the rate or range of pay that has been approved for each job in an organization; however, it does not show the actual wage rates that are paid. The pay structure provides the framework for all compensation practices in a company.

peer review organization (PRO) A group of practicing physicians and other health care professionals under contract to a company (or state or federal government) to review the care provided to employees (or Medicare patients). Typically, PROs help decide whether care is reasonable and necessary, is provided in the appropriate setting, and meets the standards of quality accepted by the medical profession.

Pension Benefit Guarantee Corporation (PBGC) An agency established by the **Employee Retirement Income Security Act of 1974** to guarantee payment of benefits to participants of **defined benefit pension plans** that meet IRS qualifications. The agency thereby became a trustee for underfunded and terminated single- and multiemployer pension plans and provides financial assistance to those plans. This assistance is funded by premiums paid by participating organizations. Participating organizations are also required to submit annual reports. In June 1990, the Supreme Court ruled that the agency could order an employer to resume its obligations for underfunded pension plans (rather than shifting liabilities to the PBGC), thereby removing a potential liability to the pension agency and causing increases in premiums from the PBGC.

pension equity plan An innovative pension design intended to provide an equitable distribution of benefits to diverse employee populations (aging **baby boomers** and mobile **baby busters**). Each year, participants are credited with a percentage of pay that will be applied to their final average earnings. The percentage increases with age, typically ranging from 4 percent for employees under 30 to 12 percent for those 60 and over. Additional percentages, typically ranging from 1 percent for participants between 35 and 39 and 3 percent for those 60 and older, are credited to earnings above the Social Security wage base to provide an additional benefit for the portion of pay not eligible for Social Security benefits. The sum of the accumulated percentages is applied to the participant's final average pay to create a lump sum value. That sum can be paid out directly to participants when they retire or leave the company. Departing employees have the option of drawing down the lump sum, converting it into an annuity, or rolling it over into an **individual retirement account** or another employer's plan. Attributed to Eric Lofgren, a consultant with the Wyatt Company, who helped develop the plan.

Pension Portability Act of 1992 (PPA) Included in legislation that extended emergency unemployment insurance benefits and signed into law by President Bush. The law, which went into effect January 1, 1993, enhances pension portability by (1) permitting direct transfers of lump sum pension payments to an **individual retirement account** (or in some cases into the plan of a new employer); (2) allowing employees to switch any portion of their benefits; and (3) giving employees advance notice of the tax advantages of a direct transfer. One provision of the law requires employers to withhold 20 percent of the withdrawal amount if the employee does not directly transfer the money into an IRA or other plan. The law was designed to encourage workers to save their retirement funds.

Pension Protection Act of 1987 (PPA) An act that increased Pension Premium Benefit Guarantee premiums, increased minimum funding for less well-funded pension plans, and reduced or eliminated the deduction of contributions for better-funded plans.

performance A basic instructional method in which the trainee is required to perform, under controlled conditions, the operation, skills, or movement being taught.

performance achievement plan A long-term, executive incentive plan in which shares of stock are awarded for the attainment of predetermined financial targets such as return on investment, growth in earnings per share, or profit. *See also* stock appreciation rights plan; stock options.

performance analysis Broad-based assessment and study of either organizational or individual performance. Performance analysis is a means of verifying significant performance deficiencies and then determining the most appropriate means of remedying those shortcomings.

performance appraisal Systematic, periodic review and analysis of employees' performance with the objective of improving that performance. Ideally, performance appraisal measures how well people do the job as compared with a set of performance standards, communicates that information to them, gets agreement on strengths and deficiencies, and results in a plan of action to enhance strengths and shore up weaknesses.

performance assessment A test that directly measures skills and abilities—such as presenting testees with appropriate materials and tools and requiring them to produce a product that meets certain specifications. Although not a new concept, performance assessment is currently being promoted as the most reliable means of assessing competency. Also called *genuine assessment, authentic evaluation,* and *practical testing. See also* alternative assessment.

performance award plan A form of executive incentive compensation plan by which formulas relating bonus distributions to selected measures of the company's financial performance are used to make payments in cash, stock, or both to executives, usually prorated according to the rank or function of the executive. *See also* employee stock option (ownership) plan; phantom stock plan.

performance-based compensation A form of incentive pay in which increases in compensation are based on the attainment of quarterly or annual targets established before the fact by the manager for individual subordinates or jointly with the subordinate. Performance-based compensation is often used in conjunction with management-by-objectives programs.

performance rating Adjectival description or numerical index used to report evaluation of job performance following observation and judgment by a qualified individual either with or without a rating scale.

performance review A less negative term to describe what has traditionally been called performance appraisal. The purpose of performance review is to improve employee performance rather than judge or rate it.

performance share plan (PSP) A stock plan that specifies the attainment of certain predetermined performance objectives before the employee has rights to the stock. The employee pays income taxes on the fair market value of the stock at the time it is issued, but can sell the stock at any time because there are no holding period restrictions.

performance shares A type of incentive plan in which shares in an organization are awarded to top managers based on how well the company does rather than how long the executive survives in his or her position of power. *See also* restricted stock plan.

performance standards 1. In employee performance appraisal, the yardsticks used to measure efficiency and effectiveness in performing a **job, duty,** or **task. 2.** In job performance measures, criteria that define the amount of time and resources required under normal conditions to complete one unit of job or task output and the characteristics of the product from the standpoint of quality.

performance support system (PSS) A system that gives users access, via workstations, to the information, guidance, assistance, and other tools they need to learn how to do their jobs and improve their productivity. Sometimes referred to as *interactive performance accelerators. See also* interactive performance system.

performance technology (PT) Systematic approaches to the improvement of human performance on the job; for example, training, organization development, incentives, job redesign, job aids, instructional technology, and ergonomics—interventions that produce results that benefit the organization.

performance test A test that requires the testee to perform a physical or mental skill that is one of the duties, tasks, or elements of a job under conditions similar or identical to those of the work environment. Includes instruments that require the testee to demonstrate some practical application, skill, or operation that is an essential part of a job or task. Sometimes, some kind of apparatus, equipment, or material is involved. The testee's performance is observed and evaluated in accordance with a predetermined standard of performance and/or product of performance. *See also* competency-based test; criterion measure; diagnostic test.

performance unit plan (PUP) A stock plan that grants units to an executive that can be exchanged for cash payments or their equivalent in stock value at the time of the award if predetermined objectives are achieved.

permanent-equity pension plan (PEPP) A new supplemental pension concept for executive compensation. Stock, rather than cash, is used as the funding vehicle to encourage key employees to develop and keep permanent equity stakes in their company. The plan ties a portion of executive pensions to stock performance. Stock is granted based on a flat percentage of pay or begins as a small percentage of current pay and gradually increases until retirement. Participants are not permitted to sell their stock until retirement or until the desired equity position is reached.

personal adjustment counseling Counseling provided to employees to help them gain self-understanding, learn how to regulate their own lives, achieve insight into difficult experiences, learn how to use their own resources as well as the resources of the organization and the larger community, and deal with emotional stress. *See also* developmental counseling.

personal days A type of employee fringe benefit. Workers are allowed a specific number of paid days off (in addition to paid holidays, annual leave, and sick leave) for any personal reason, such as attending to personal business, attending a school play, keeping a doctor's appointment, or just goofing off. Some employers allow workers to use their personal days on an hourly rather than a full-day basis.

personality and temperament test Usually referred to as personality profiles, inventories, schedules, or scales, personality and temperament tests are used in business and industry to evaluate personality in normal adults and predict human behavior in business for career planning, selection, job placement, promotion, and counseling. They purport to measure some dimension of human personality or temperament, such as whether a person is withdrawn or outgoing, a team player or a loner, mature or immature, emotionally stable or unstable, passive or aggressive, and they are projective in that they disclose a person's needs and values. These tests are usually reserved for the task of selecting individuals for executive or professional positions. They should be administered and interpreted by qualified psychometrists, psychologists, or therapists. Examples are Gordon Personal Profile-Inventory, Edwards Personal Preference Schedule, California Psychological Inventory, Wonderlic Comprehensive Personality Profile, Thurston Temperament Schedule, Taylor Sales Attitudes Checklist, and Jenkins Activity Survey.

phantom stock plan The least common of the various forms of long-term incentives, usually limited to the top 2 or 3 percent of exempt employees. Phantom stock plans provide payments in cash or in stock based on hypothetical investments in company stock equal to the gain in fair market value of a designated number of company shares ascribed to each participant in the plan on the date of the grant. Future payments may be based on future appreciation, initial value plus future appreciation, or may provide dividend equivalent payments. Also called *stock appreciation rights plan*. *See also* capital accumulation plan; performance award plan; restricted stock plan.

phased retirement A plan for keeping older workers on the payroll for an agreed-upon length of time, at least in a part-time capacity, as an effective way to keep longtime employees, strengthen the role of older workers, and help compensate for the growing shortage of workers. *See also* flexiplace; work sharing.

physical and mental impairment As defined by the **Americans with Disabilities Act of 1990,** "physical or mental impairment includes, but is not limited to, such contagious and noncontagious diseases and conditions as orthopedic, visual, speech, and hearing impairments, cerebral palsy, epilepsy, muscular dystrophy, multiple sclerosis, cancer, heart disease, diabetes, mental retardation, emotional illness, specific learning disabilities, HIV disease (whether symptomatic or asymptomatic), tuberculosis, drug addiction, and alcoholism." (It does not include homosexuality or bisexuality).

physically disabled Includes people who are totally or partially deaf, totally or partially blind, those having speech problems, orthopedically handicapped people (loss of normal use of limbs, bones, or muscles due to disease, injury, or deformity, such as cerebral palsy, muscular dystrophy, congenital deformities, and amputation), and those having health or medical problems (such as AIDS, asthma, epilepsy, diabetes, and heart conditions).

physician profiling A means of **utilization review** in which companies track physicians' patterns of practice to reduce the costs of either inpatient or outpatient care.

piece rate In incentive piecework, the rate paid to a worker per piece produced or worked on. *See also* incentive work.

piecework *See* piece rate; incentive work.

pink-collar workers Women who work in low-paying jobs that are in many cases equivalent to higher-paying white-collar jobs typically filled by men.

pink slip An oral or written notice of discharge, firing, layoff, or termination (either for cause, downsizing, or restructuring).

place of public accommodation As defined by the **Americans with Disabilities Act of 1990,** "a facility, operated by a private entity, whose operations affect commerce and fall within at least one of 12 specified categories." Includes (1) places of lodging; (2) establishments serving food or drink; (3) places of exhibition or entertainment; (4) places of public gathering; (5) sales or rental establishments; (6) service establishments; (7) stations used for specified public transportation; (8) places of public display or collection; (9) places of recreation; (10) places of education; (11) social service center establishments; and (12) places of exercise or recreation.

platform hours An instructor work load measure. The number of hours per day or per week that an instructor is interacting with trainees in an instructional setting. Most collective bargaining agreements establish a maximum number of platform hours per week for instructors.

platform preparation factor A measure of instructor work load. The relationship between the number of hours an instructor can teach a specific block of instruction (determined by the **platform-to-preparation-time ratio**) and the total number of teaching hours available per day.

platform-to-preparation-time ratio The amount of preparation time allowed (or required by contract) per hour of instruction. It varies with such factors as the complexity of the content, availability of reference materials, amount of research required, and number of times the block of instruction is repeated.

play or pay model An approach to health care reform in which employers would be required either to provide health insurance or pay a special payroll tax surcharge to finance a public system that would cover their employees. One plan would require businesses with twenty-five or more employees to provide coverage or pay a 7 percent payroll tax for uninsured employees, and a federal board would monitor fees and simplify the claims process. *See also* managed competition plan.

point-factor method An approach to **job evaluation** in which the desired hierarchical classification of jobs in an organization is achieved by identifying **compensable factors** and assigning to each one scores or points indicating increasing degrees of intensity, scope, difficulty, or value. Each job is then assessed in terms of the appropriate degree for each compensable factor, and separate scores are summed to yield a final point score for that job. *See also* factor comparison; job classification; job ranking.

point-of-service (POS) A type of managed care. Consists of a formal network of primary care physicians, organized by insurers, who serve as **gatekeepers** to the services of other health care providers (specialists, hospitals, and so on). For those using physicians on the point of service list of approved providers, a low fee, with no deductible, is charged. For using other providers, the charges are higher in terms of deductibles and coinsurance.

pooling A flexible benefit plan option in which employees are allowed to draw as needed from an account that combines vacation, holiday, sick, and personal paid time off. *See also* flexible benefits/flex benefits program; paid time off.

population comparison A means of determining or proving adverse impact (discrimination) in screening and selection. Population comparison involves comparing the percentage of an organization's minority group employees and the percentage of that minority in the general population in the surrounding community. It is an error-prone method because of the difficulty of defining the relevant labor market. *See also* disparate impact.

portable pension A pension plan that allows workers who change jobs to have their benefits rolled over into **individual retirement accounts,** allowing workers to withdraw funds from a **defined contribution plan** as taxable cash, or shifting retirement funds between employers (an uncommon and possibly undesirable practice). *See also* rollover.

Portal-to-Portal Act of 1947 (PTPA) An act designed to correct judicial interpretations of the **Fair Labor Standards Act of 1938,** the **Walsh-Healy Public Contracts Act of 1936,** and the **Davis-Bacon Act of 1931** in disregard of long-standing customs and practices between employers and employees. Specifically the Act relieves employers from liability and punishment under the cited laws for failing to pay minimum wages or overtime compensation to employees engaged in walking, riding, or traveling to and from the workplace or area in which the principal activities for which the worker was employed to perform are conducted and for activities that are preliminary to or postliminary to the principal activity or activities. Exceptions include express provisions of a written or nonwritten contract or a custom or practice in effect at the time of such activity between the employee, his or her agent, the collective bargaining unit and the employer.

preadmission review (PAR) A requirement for certification of medical necessity before an employee can be admitted to a hospital for surgery or other medical treatment. Involves assessment of the appropriateness of in-hospital treatment and the duration of such treatment. PAR typically includes psychiatric and substance abuse as well as other hospital admissions.

preadmission testing (PAT) A plan that allows employees planning to be hospitalized, usually for a surgical procedure, to have certain tests, such as X rays, blood tests, and other presurgical tests, performed on an outpatient basis prior to admission.

preauthorization A requirement of health maintenance organizations, preferred provider organizations, and other providers to evaluate the necessity of certain costly medical and surgical procedures before they are performed. Preauthorization is used to determine whether the procedure is necessary, eliminate unnecessary expense, and help patients avoid the costs, pain, and risks associated with such procedures. Examples are angiography, laminectomy, knee arthroscopy, upper gastrointestinal endoscopy, and hemorrhoidectomy. Also called *precertification.*

preferred provider organization (PPO) A health care organization comprising medical groups, physicians, or hospitals, under contract with corporations to provide medical or other health care products and services. In exchange for guaranteeing a certain volume of employee referrals from their companies, employers are granted discount rates from the providers and are thereby provided better control of costs. PPOs are also seen by employers as a means of monitoring the quality and quantity of health care. *See also* health maintenance organization; open-ended health maintenance organization.

Pregnancy Discrimination Act of 1978 (PDA) An amendment to **Title VII** of the **Civil Rights Act of 1964.** Prohibits discrimination in employment practices, including disability, sick leave, and health care benefits, on the bases of pregnancy, childbirth, or related medical conditions. Essentially, the Act requires an employer to treat a woman unable to work because of pregnancy-related conditions exactly the same as any other employee unable to work for other reasons and to provide health care coverage for pregnancy on the same basis as for other medical conditions. It is a violation of PDA to require pregnant women to take leaves of mandatory duration unless a similar requirement is imposed on male employees with disabilities that impair their job performance. However, a mandatory leave policy that affects solely pregnant women may be justified by **business necessity**. *See also* discrimination; fetal protection policy.

premium pay Extra pay, in addition to regular wages or salary, for work performed outside or in addition to regularly scheduled work periods, such as Sundays, holidays, nights, and so on.

prepaid health care organization An organization such as a health maintenance organization or competitive medical plan that receives direct payments from the insurance carrier (or Medicare) for the services it provides to subscribers.

prepaid legal plan A relatively new taxable employee benefit. May include a legal insurance policy, similar to medical insurance plans offered by health maintenance organizations. Other plans feature unlimited phone advice from and consultation with an attorney by employees and members of their families, will preparation, legal document review, legal representation in the form of letters or phone calls made by an attorney, and referral services for more involved legal counsel. Few plans include representation by an attorney in court cases.

prepayment health plan A health care plan by which health care providers, such as health maintenance organization and competitive medical plans, are paid on a monthly basis for each covered beneficiary.

prescription drug plan (PDP) A benefits plan in which all or a part (percentage) of the costs of employees' prescription drugs are paid by the insurer.

prevailing charge A fee based on the customary charges for covered medical insurance services or items. It is also the maximum charge Medicare can approve for any item or service.

prevailing wage rate The amount typically paid by employers in a labor market or geographical area for similar work. *See also* Davis-Bacon Acts of 1931 and 1964; McNamara-O'Hara Service Contract Act of 1965.

primary care provider A health care practitioner, such as a physician, who takes care of all medical needs short of subspecialty care and surgery. For example, a primary care physician performs physical exams, treats diabetic-related ailments, heart problems, hypertension, and stress-related problems, and counsels patients in a variety of areas.

prioritization of resources A means of determining the level of health care benefits, in terms of which services or therapies should be made available to Americans. Methodologies currently used or in prospect include medical effectiveness of a service (clinical outcomes) and patient characteristics (such as employment potential or income).

Privacy Act of 1974 (PA) A law designed to protect people against invasions of privacy by federal agencies. Applies to all federal agencies and private firms that keep records for a federal agency under contract. The Act permits individuals to decide what records kept by an agency or department are important and to insist that they be used only for the purpose for which the information was collected. The individual also has the right to see the information accompanied by a person of his or her own choice, file information to correct mistakes, amend and add details, dispute records they believe to be inaccurate, and make or be provided a copy of all or any portion of a record in a comprehensive form upon request and payment of a reasonable fee that excludes the costs of research or review. The law also requires that records be maintained showing to whom disclosures (other than internal uses) were made and that they be retained for at least five years or the life of the record, whichever is longer. Doubtful requests for information must be referred to legal counsel, the privacy officer, or a senior executive for decision. Reasonable administrative, technical, and physical safeguards must be established to ensure protection against inadvertent disclosure and ensure disclosure only to authorized personnel with a need to know.

See also Fair Credit Reporting Act of 1969; Freedom of Information Act of 1966.

professional development 1. A continuing and deliberate organization-sponsored process aimed at assisting, encouraging, and enabling professionals as individuals to improve their performance and potential—developing their knowledge, skills, abilities, and values. **2.** The process of keeping current in one's occupation or profession, maintaining competence in one's practice, and remaining open to new theories, techniques, and approaches.

proficiency test A test that indicates relative levels of performance or achievement whether in adjectival (poor, fair, good, or excellent) or numerical (raw, standard, percentile, T, or stanine) scores. Although a cut or passing score may be established for them, proficiency tests essentially establish relative ranks or standings on the tasks or information tested.

profile A graphic representation of test results on several tests for either an individual or group using identical or comparable measures such as standard scores and percentile ranks.

profit-sharing plan Deferred compensation established and maintained to provide for the participation of employees or their beneficiaries in company profits. Profit-sharing plans are **defined contribution plans** that are employer-funded and contributions are flexible; that is, the amount of the contribution can be changed annually. They do not guarantee a fixed level of benefits; however, to meet qualification requirements they must provide a definite predetermined formula for allocating the contributions and distributing the funds after a fixed number of years, on attainment of a stated age, or occurrence of layoff, illness, disability, retirement, termination of employment, or death. Maximum annual contribution for each employee is 15 percent of gross compensation up to a limit of $30,000; for self-employed persons the maximum is 13.04 percent of net self-employment income. *See also* capital accumulation plan; money-purchase pension plan.

progression chart A document that depicts planned progression, including alternative routes, from the lowest to the highest positions in specific career fields or in an organization. In some cases, the chart shows progression to positions in other elements of the organization. Progression charts are used as source documents for planning and designing training and development programs, building an in-house source of candidates for vacated or newly established positions, and motivating people by identifying specific opportunities for advancement to more challenging and remunerative positions. *See also* career ladder.

prospective payment system In benefits, a process started in 1983 under which hospitals are paid fixed amounts on the principal diagnosis for each Medicare hospital stay based on payment categories called **diagnosis-related groups.**

protected characteristics A legal term that relates to areas protected by statutes. For example, that an action, program, or requirement conflicts with a person's religious beliefs or discriminates against them or that their privacy has been or will be violated. People can object on some protected ground. *See also* Age Discrimination in Employment Act of 1967; Americans with Disabilities Act of 1990; job-relatedness; Title VII.

protected class A legal term used to describe women and minorities (African-Americans, Native Americans, Alaskan natives, Asians, Pacific Islanders, Hispanics, people over 40, disabled persons, and Vietnam-era veterans) who are specifically "protected" from discrimination by the law or court decisions interpreting the law. *See also* adverse impact, equal employment opportunity; Title VII.

protection benefits Benefits awarded on a contingency basis only, such as accident, illness, injury, disability, or death. Examples are medical and hospitalization insurance, dental and vision care plans, life insurance, sick leave, and safety equipment and clothing. *See also* benefits, entitlements; equity benefits; statutory benefits.

provider An organization or individual that provides medical services and supplies under an agreement or contract (such as a **health maintenance organization** or **preferred provider organization**). Providers include physicians and other health care professionals, hospitals, ambulatory surgical centers, physical and occupational therapists, clinical laboratories, X-ray suppliers, dialysis facilities, and rural health clinics.

psychological test A test instrument used to screen, select, and assign employees, select employees for promotion and for training and development, classify and group trainees, determine the effectiveness and quality of instructional systems, provide a basis for guiding and assisting employees in career development and trainees in improving their performance, diagnose mental and emotional problems and illnesses, and keep management informed about progress and results. Includes tests of mental ability, aptitude, spatial reasoning, psychomotor skills, interests, and personality and temperament.

psychomotor domain 1. Applied to learning, the learner's physical skills and abilities. **2.** A classification of instructional objectives that focuses on motor skills. *See also* affective domain; cognitive domain.

Q

QC   Quality circle.

QCM   Quality of care measurement.

qualified plan A defined benefit and defined contribution pension or profit-sharing plan that qualifies under statutory requirements and IRS regulations for certain tax advantages, usually accruing to both the employer and the employee. Generally, qualification is dependent upon a determination that the plan does not discriminate in favor of highly compensated employees.

qualified retirement plan Tax-advantaged means of accumulating retirement dollars, the plans come in several forms: traditional **defined benefit pension plans, defined contribution plans,** and 401(k) plans. The term "qualified" means that the plans are eligible for special tax treatment by both employers and employees.

quality circle (QC) A participative management technique. A quality circle consists of a carefully selected homogeneous group of employees who meet regularly for an hour or two each week to consider specific problems and develop recommendations for solutions for presentation to management. Knowledge workers should focus on problems relating to internal departmental and external organizational functions, relationships, and services and performance and quality of work life programs.

quality of care measurement (QCM) In health benefits, a program to determine what employees are getting from a **utilization review** system—a means of measuring and achieving quality control and cost-containment.

quota strategy or system An affirmative action initiative involving steps to achieve balance in an organization by mandating hiring and promotion restrictions that favor protected groups. It also includes the risk of being sued for reverse discrimination. *See also* good faith effort strategy or system; reverse bias or discrimination.

R

RA	Rehabilitation Act of 1973.
REA	Retirement Equity Act of 1984.
RIF	Reduction in force.
RRA	Revenue Reconciliation Act of 1990.
RRP	Resource referral program.
RTK	Right-to-know.

rabbi trust A supplemental pension benefit plan in the form of a trust fund that allows executives to avoid being taxed on income earned by the trust until they begin receiving payments at retirement. *See also* secular trust.

race-norming The practice of adjusting scores on employment or job-placement tests to compensate for racial differences. For example, the scores of African-Americans and Hispanics on employment tests sometimes have been segregated by racial groups, compared only with their own racial group, and reported not in relation to all those taking the test, but only in relation to others in the individual's racial group. That is, scores are ranked using one of three available scales: one for African-Americans, one for Hispanics, and one for whites and others. As a result, the percentile scores of minorities are increased. The practice was in use for more than 10 years and was commonly applied in about 34 states and by some private employers. The practice was prohibited by the **Civil Rights Act of 1991** because it banned any consideration of race or sex in employment decisions. The ban was implemented on December 15, 1991, by an administration announcement that state employment agencies could no longer increase the scores of minority applicants on one federally sanctioned aptitude test (used for low-level manufacturing or clerical jobs measuring skills like math, reading, and manual dexterity) to raise scores. Other test scores are almost certain to be covered by the same prohibition. However, the Civil

Rights Act does allow the use of "lawful affirmative action" programs, so the ban is likely to generate lawsuits as African-Americans and Hispanics find themselves dropped from job referral lists.

rate buster An individual worker who violates a work team's norms by producing more than his or her fellow workers. Such employees are usually ostracized by the group.

rationed care A controversial cost containment strategy that involves the establishment of a "global budget" for all health care delivered in a region, state, or nation. It limits the availability of specialists and sophisticated medical procedures by establishing a list of services, such as treatment for incurable diseases and infertility therapy, for which state- or federally-sponsored insurance will not provide reimbursement. Currently, only the state of Oregon has federal approval for its Medicaid health care allocation plan.

reasonable accommodation 1. A legal term relating to measures an employer must take to "accommodate" an employee's objections to an action, requirement, or program on job-relatedness or protected grounds to avoid a lawsuit. **2.** A requirement of the **Americans with Disabilities Act of 1990** with respect to hiring or making workplace adjustments for disabled persons: modifying work schedules, restructuring jobs, making physical modifications to the work area, installing special equipment, providing an interpreter or reader. In the case of operating a public establishment, reasonable accommodation for people with disabilities would also include removing structural barriers, providing auxiliary aids and services, and modifying policies, rules, and procedures.

reasonable charge In health care benefits, the amount that is usually charged for the same or similar services or treatment in the same service area. However, reasonable charges are usually construed as the amount approved by insurance carriers, which is typically either the customary charge, the prevailing charge, or the actual charge, whichever is the lowest.

reasonable investigation A legal doctrine that pertains to inquiries relating to a job applicant's fitness for a job, such as preemployment medical examinations, screening for physical disabilities, genetic testing, and so on. It requires that reviews and inquiries be proper, legitimate, and justifiable.

reasonable rule or order A legal doctrine that pertains to determinations of wrongful discharge. In effect, it asks, "Is the employer's rule or order reasonably related to the orderly, efficient, and safe operation of the business and the performance the employer has a right to expect?"

reasonable woman standard A new test that expands the definition of

sexual harassment in the workplace. Essentially, the standard asks: "Would a reasonable *woman* consider the alleged act or action to be sexually harassing or intimidating?"

reciprocal review An appraisal system in which the performances of both the manager and the subordinate are evaluated. The subordinate evaluates the manager and the manager evaluates the subordinate based on performance criteria agreed to in advance by both parties. They jointly determine progress and accomplishment, identify shortfalls, and establish action plans.

recycling The practice of requiring a trainee to repeat a module or an entire course of instruction because of inadequate performance.

redeployment Reassigning workers to openings in other functional areas, departments, or branches, rather than laying them off. *See also* implacement.

reduction in force (RIF) A common consequence of or accompaniment to downsizing—the layoff of employees. That is, voluntary or involuntary termination of employees as a response to competitive pressures, economic downturns, mergers and takeovers, and downsizing and restructuring. Voluntary RIFs usually include financial inducements and other early retirement incentives. Involuntary RIFs are simply layoffs.

reentry training 1. Training provided to individuals who, for one reason or another (illness, injury, child rearing, and so on) have been out of the work force for an extended period of time and need either initial or refresher training in the skills and knowledge required by the job. 2. Training provided to returnees from extended overseas assignments to help them adjust to the culture shock when they return to the United States.

referral agent program A form of employee assistance program in which a person is selected and given brief and minimum training and information about available community counseling services. The agent's responsibilities are limited to listening to the employee's diagnosis of his or her problem and referring the individual to an appropriate source of help, usually a public agency. *See also* in-company diagnosis.

Rehabilitation Act of 1973 (RA) An act designed to develop and implement comprehensive and coordinated programs of vocational rehabilitation for persons with handicaps to maximize their employability, independence, and integration into the workplace and community by assisting them to obtain employment and secure on-the-job accommodations following hiring. It applied to government contractors and subcontractors, recipients of federal aid, and government employees. The Act proscribed discrimination on the basis of disability in local programs and activities benefiting from federal financial assistance. Enforcement has improved program accessibility for disabled persons to health care, social services, recreation, housing, and transportation and opened educational opportunities to disabled persons at all levels. The Act also proscribed barriers to the employment of people with disabilities in the screening and selection processes, particularly during the employment interview. The Act mandated affirmative action to hire handicapped individuals and treat them fairly, including making workplace modifications. The amendments of 1974 created the Architectural Barriers Compliance Board, which monitors compliance with the **Architectural Barriers Act of 1968**. *See also* Rehabilitation Act Amendments of 1992.

Rehabilitation Act Amendments of 1992 Legislation designed to embed the precepts and values of the **Americans with Disabilities Act of 1990** into the **Rehabilitation Act of 1973** and extend the Act through 1997. The amendments revise the Act to develop and implement, through research, training, services, and the guarantee of equal opportunity, comprehensive and coordinated programs of vocational rehabilitation and independent living for individuals with disabilities to maximize their employment, independence, and integration into the workplace and the community.

reimbursement account An option of most **flexible benefits programs** (plans), in which eligible expenses are reimbursed on a nontaxable basis. Contributions to these accounts come from two sources: employer residual flexible benefits dollars and employee salary deductions. There are two types of reimbursement accounts allowed by the Internal Revenue Service (health care and dependent day care) but only if the following rules are met: (1) annual employee election of the amount of contribution(s); (2) nontransferability of funds; (3) forfeiture of unused funds; and (4) a contribution limit for day care (determined by the employer) of up to $5,000 per year for married employees who file jointly or those who are single, and $2,500 for employees who are married but filing separately. *See also* day care reimbursement account; health care reimbursement account.

release agreement Primarily a means of protecting an organization against unlawful discharge suits. However, release agreements are also designed to avoid litigation between an employer and an employee or consultant, a maker and a distributor, or a producer and talent (actors) or other performers. A release agreement is a clearly written legal document executed by either or both parties. In the case of employer-employee releases, they are usually signed by the employee in exchange for some benefit from the employer that the employer is not obligated to give following the employee's discharge, resignation, or layoff. In exchange for the benefit, the employee gives up all claims against the employer in connection with the employment, including termination or resignation.

reliability A measure of the ability of a psychological test, achievement test, rating scale, or other instrument of appraisal to evaluate consistently whatever is being measured. Expressed as a coefficient of reliability. *See also* validity.

relocation allowance A lump-sum payment to domestic transfers or foreign-based employees to cover such things as remodeling living quarters, purchasing furnishings, and obtaining licenses and permits.

relocation assistance Pretransfer and posttransfer assistance provided to domestic or overseas transfers, such as providing information (briefings, information packages, and individual counseling) on such matters as tax and insurance forms required, critical policies and procedures, pay and benefits, and sources of assistance, and getting relocation payments to the individual, helping with the move, and so on.

remedial training Repeat training and guided practice provided to remedy or correct deficiencies in trainee performance. It is given *when* it is needed. Remedial training may be provided to groups or to individuals, one-on-one.

remote employee An employee who (1) works at a site removed from his or her supervisor, or (2) is under contract and works on "secret" projects to which his or her supervisor does not have access.

rent-a-judge An **alternative dispute resolution procedure** in which the parties to the controversy agree to employ a judge, usually a retired jurist, to render an opinion on the dispute. The opinion may be either binding or nonbinding. *See also* arbitration; fact-finding; med-arb; mediation, mini-trial; summary jury trial.

resource-based relative value scale (RBRVS) A Medicare cost reduction strategy passed by Congress in 1989 that changes the way health care providers are paid for their services. The results of a Harvard research study that forms the basis for new Medicare physician payment legislation that began in 1992 and will become fully operational in 1996. It replaces the current "usual, customary, and reasonable" reimbursement system with uniform national set fees based on such variables as the practitioner's time, effort, training and skill, as well as office overhead. Under RBRVS, physicians with family medicine, pediatric, and internist practices will receive higher fees than formerly and doctors practicing more invasive medicine (such as heart, thoracic, and orthopedic surgery) will receive lower fees than currently. Under the system, such physician services as taking medical histories and counseling patients will be valued as highly as surgical procedures. Congress is considering expanding the application of RBRVS to private insurance beginning in 1994. *See also* diagnosis-related groups.

resource referral program (RRP) Usually contracted by an employer to assist employees in locating dependent-care services.

respondeat superior Literally, "let the master respond." An employment doctrine that holds an employer liable for his or her employees' negligent on-the-job actions and does not depend in any way on the plaintiff's ability to prove the employer's negligence. *See also* negligent hiring; negligent job references.

restatement of tort An advisory standard used by the courts in liability cases. Essentially it states that anyone who, in the course of his or her business, profession, or employment, supplies false information to others to guide them in their business transactions is subject to liability for monetary loss to them by their reliance on the information provided, if the provider fails to exercise reasonable care in communicating the information. The standard also states that "Communications between employers regarding the previous work history and character of an employee are protected from claims of defamation if the statements are made in 'good faith.'" Therefore, although an employer cannot deliberately submit false information about a former or current employee in response to a request from a prospective employer, he or she is protected from claims of defamation if the statements are made in "good faith." *See also* negligent hiring.

restricted stock plan A form of long-term executive incentive plan that provides the employee with the benefits of stock ownership in the form of dividends; however, restrictions are placed on the disposal of such stock (usually that it revert back to the corporation). *See also* employee stock option (ownership) plan; performance award plan; performance shares; phantom stock plan; stock appreciation rights plan.

restrictive policy Prima facie evidence of discrimination in that it demonstrates that an employer (intentionally or unintentionally) has been using a hiring policy or procedure to exclude members of a protected group. For example, a policy against hiring women for assembly line jobs or against hiring women with young children.

retaliatory discharge A form of workplace discrimination: discharge designed to punish workers for certain actions. Illegal in most states where, for example, statutes have been enacted to prohibit termination of employees filing for workers' compensation benefits. *See also* termination-at-will.

retiree skill bank A cost-effective means of attracting skilled and experienced employees and an attractive option for former employees who want to continue to work. A retiree skill bank is a temporary pool of retired employees who are rehired by their former employer on an occasional, temporary, or contractual basis.

Retirement Equity Act of 1984 (REA) An act that liberalized **Employee Retirement Income Security Act of 1974's** participation, vesting, and service requirements. It extends preretirement surviving spouse protection to all vested employees. The Act also requires employers to obtain written consent from spouses of retiring workers who choose pension benefits payable only during their lifetimes rather than a joint and survivor plan. A General Accounting Office study recommended that consent forms be written in nontechnical language and include clear explanations of the effects of the consent on the worker's annuity.

Revenue Reconciliation Act of 1990 (RRA) Includes provisions for a new tax credit for barrier removal in existing buildings to specifically comply with the **Americans with Disabilities Act of 1990.**

reverse bias or discrimination In affirmative action plans, particularly with quota systems, charges by the plaintiff that unfair preferences were accorded minorities in hiring, promotion, or layoff situations. *See also* quota strategy or system.

right-to-act Legislation pursued at both federal and state levels that would give workers more authority to refuse to perform duties they believe would put them at risk of serious injury.

right-to-know (RTK) Occupational Safety and Health Administration standards established to protect the health and safety of workers, including those in nonmanufacturing organizations, by keeping them informed of the dangerous substances with which they are working, the hazards and symptoms. Legislation directs that employers inform their employees of hazardous conditions, chemicals, vapors, and the like. A major provision of the standard requires employee training in chemical safety. *See also* Bloodborne Pathogens Standard; Hazard Communication Standard of 1988; Laboratory Chemical Standard.

right-to-work Legislation underscoring the right of employees to work. Twenty-one states now have "right-to-work" laws that prohibit mandatory union membership. *See also* Fair Labor Standards Act of 1938.

risk rating Used by insurance carriers to ensure fairness to all who apply for health insurance coverage, particularly those with lower health risks. Direct risk rating (also called medical underwriting) involves evaluating applicants for insurance to identify those with medical problems whose coverage is reduced or their premiums increased. Insurers may also exclude entire industries or drop specific groups of workers when their claims become large. Indirect risk rating involves the imposition of waiting periods, copayments, payment ceilings, and the exclusion of certain procedures, tests, or drugs. The practice is condemned by some as systematic discrimination against disadvantaged minorities, older workers, and people with chronic conditions. It is lauded by others who see it as a more equitable system in which risk is assigned to the responsible individual rather than pooled among insureds. *See also* cherry picking.

risk-sharing arrangement A managed care contract that stipulates that both the insured and the insurer share the risks and potential for gain. May involve rate guarantees depending on the size and clout of an employer's preferred provider network, the performance of the managed care program, inflation of medical costs, changing technology, and utilization patterns.

rollover Transfer of funds from one account to another without tax penalty. For example, federal taxes on lump-sum distributions can be deferred (or avoided) by placing them in a rollover individual retirement account. Or if an individual is changing jobs, a rollover IRA (also called a *conduit IRA*) can serve as a temporary tax-deferred investment vehicle until the distribution is moved to the qualified plan of a new employer. Once funds are withdrawn from an IRA, the IRS allows only 60 days after receipt to reinvest assets in a new IRA. Assets not reinvested within that period are considered a taxable distribution and, if the individual has not reached age 59½, is not disabled, and does not fall within certain other exemptions, there is also a 10 percent early withdrawal penalty. Only one rollover is allowed per year. *See also* individual retirement account; portable pension.

rotator An employee who works changing shifts; e.g, changing periodically from 7 to 3, to 3 to 11, and 11 to 7 (graveyard shift). Such schedules are believed to disturb circadian rhythms (the body clock), increase stress in employees at work and at home, and result in fatigue, health problems, irritability, reduced job performance, lower productivity, and higher accident rates.

Rule of 75 In early retirement programs, where the basis for eligibility is established as any combination of age and years of service totaling 75 or more.

S

SADLs	Significant activities of daily living.
SAR	1. Stock appreciation rights plan. 2. Summary annual report.
SARA	Superfund Amendments and Reauthorization Act of 1986.
SAR-SEP	Salary reduction-simplified employee pension.
SCANS	Secretary's Commission on Achieving Necessary Skills.
SEP	Simplified employee pension.
SEPPA	Single Employer Pension Plan Amendments Act of 1986.
SERP	Supplemental executive retirement plan.
SIBP	Self-insured benefits plan.
SIG	Self-insurance group.
SMA	Self-managed account.
SMHMO	Staff model health maintenance organization.
SPD	Summary plan description.
SSA	Social Security Act of 1935.
SSI	Supplemental Security Income.
SSO	Second surgical opinion.
SUB	Supplemental unemployment benefits.

Safe Harbor Regulations Regulations issued by the Department of Labor on September 3, 1987, to interpret the requirements of Section 404(c) of the **Employee Retirement Income Security Act of 1974**. In brief, the regulations offer employers relief from fiduciary responsibility for investment performance if they offer each participant in individual account plans a range of investment options, an opportunity to invest the assets in his or her account in a "safe" investment, and control over assets.

salary-based deductible Health care coverage that ties the deductible to salary—to ability to pay. That is, the deductible increases for those who can afford to pay and decreases for those who cannot.

salary compression A consequence of inflation. The symptoms of salary compression are higher salaries for new hires than for current workers, and hourly pay increases for workers that have matched or overtaken supervisory compensation levels.

salary grade A level of compensation, usually a **salary range** and not an individual amount, established for a group of similar jobs.

salary range A band of salaries, from minimum to maximum, set for a specific job.

salary reduction-simplified employee pension (SAR-SEP) A retirement plan in which employees may contribute to their retirement through an IRA. In companies with 25 or fewer employees, the employees make pretax contributions, as with a Section 401(k) plan. Employees may contribute up to $7,313 (adjusted annually for cost of living) of their pretax earnings, provided at least 50 percent of the eligible employees choose this type of salary reduction arrangement.

sandbagging Where executive compensation is directly tied to business plans, the unethical practice of establishing a plan that is easily achieved in order to win a large raise or bonus.

savings and thrift plan A type of **defined contribution plan** in which an employee's contributions to a pension plan are matched in whole or in part by the employer. *See also* deferred profit-sharing plan.

savings plan A type of pension plan in which employees set aside a fixed percentage of their weekly wages or salary for their retirement; the company usually matches from 50 to 100 percent of the employee's contribution. *See also* group pension plan.

school matching A service offered to employees as a benefit by a growing number of companies. The service helps employees find schools that match the needs of their children. Initially offered to families who were relocating and wanted to buy homes in an area with good schools, the service is now offered to all employees to enhance recruitment, retention, and morale.

second surgical opinion (SSO) An opinion provided by an independent physician, a requirement of many company medical and health benefits plans, such as health maintenance organizations, designed to prevent unnecessary surgery or other therapy or reduce or contain costs.

Secretary's Commission on Achieving Necessary Skills (SCANS) A 31-member commission formed by the Secretary of Labor in 1990 to identify the skills needed by employees in a high-performance workplace. The report of the commission, "Learning a Living: A Blueprint for High Performance," published in 1992, called for a partnership of employers, schools, parents, and government to make education more relevant to the needs of the future work force.

Section 44, Internal Revenue Code Allows an eligible small business (with annual gross receipts under $1 million) to elect a nonrefundable tax credit equal to 50 percent of the amount of eligible disability access expenditures for any tax year between $259 and $10,250; consequently the maximum amount of the credit for any taxable year is $5,000. An "eligible small business" is defined as any person or corporation that (1) had gross receipts (reduced by returns and allowances) for the preceding taxable year that did not exceed $1 million or (2) had no more than 30 full-time employees, and (3) elects the application of the disabled access credit for the tax year. An employee is considered full-time if employed at least 30 hours per week for 20 or more calendar weeks in the tax year. Eligible access expenditures include amounts paid or incurred: (1) to remove architectural, communication, physical, or transportation barriers; (2) to provide qualified interpreters or other means of making aurally delivered materials available to individuals with hearing impairments; (3) to provide qualified readers, taped texts, and other methods of making visually delivered materials available to individuals with visual impairments; (4) to acquire or modify equipment or devices for individuals with disabilities; or (5) to provide other similar services, modifications, materials, or equipment.

Section 89, Internal Revenue Code A provision of the **Tax Reform Act of 1986,** which made benefits received by employees taxable unless employer-provided benefit plans met certain nondiscrimination requirements set out by the IRS as Section 89, Internal Revenue Code. The intent of the Act was to avoid giving tax-favored status to benefit plans that benefit only highly paid employees. The Act was repealed in 1989. As a consequence, nondiscrimination and qualification rules were completely repealed; the pre-Tax Reform Act nondiscrimination rules for group term life insurance plans, self-insured medical plans, and cafeteria plans were restored; nondiscrimination rules for dependent care assistance plans, with certain changes, were retained; and relief from the separate-line-of-business rules that apply to qualified pension and profit-sharing plans was provided. Specifically, employers will have to comply with several restored parts of the Internal Revenue Code subject to nondiscrimination rules. They include Section 79 group term life policies, Section 105(h) self-insured medical reimbursement plans, Section 129 dependent care assistance programs, Section 125 cafeteria plans, and Section 505(b) benefits provided through voluntary employees' beneficiary association trusts.

Section 125, Internal Revenue Code A section of the Internal Revenue Code covering flexible or "cafeteria style" benefits plans, in which employees can choose from several different benefits to make up largely individualized benefits packages. Two types of **flexible spending account** (FSA) may be established: health care FSAs or dependent care FSAs. FSAs begin when an employee authorizes contributions to one or both types of accounts. Contributions to these accounts remain tax-exempt for all federal and most state and local taxes. *See also* cafeteria plan.

Section 127, Internal Revenue Code The section of the Internal Revenue Code (Employee Educational Assistance) that made employer-provided tuition reimbursement a tax-free benefit. The Employee Educational Assistance tuition-reimbursement tax exclusion, which was due to expire December 30, 1991, was reauthorized until June 30, 1992, by the Congress and signed into law by President Bush. EEAA allows workers to deduct employer-paid tuition reimbursements from their gross income up to a limit of $5,250 per year for non-job-related courses. *See* Employee Educational Assistance Act of 1978.

Section 190, Internal Revenue Code Allows an annual tax deduction of up to $15,000 by any taxpayer who removes barriers to people with disabilities in a place where a business or trade is conducted, including places of public accommodation and transportation systems. The deduction applies only to the removal of barriers at existing places of business or trade. To qualify for the deduction, the modification must conform with design standards issued by the U.S. Architectural and Transportation Barriers Compliance Board and the Uniform Federal Accessibility Standard. *See also* Section 44, Internal Revenue Code.

Section 401(k), Internal Revenue Code Deals with employee investment plans as modified by the **Tax Reform Act of 1986.** A type of **defined contribution plan** providing retirement or salary deferral benefits also known as cash or deferred arrangements. Such plans can be funded entirely by the employee, entirely by the employer, or jointly by both. Combined employer and employee contributions are limited to 20 percent of gross annual compensation to a maximum of $30,000, including annual employee contributions of up to $7,313 (adjusted yearly for cost of living) on a pretax basis. Employer contributions are deductible from current income, and both employer and employee contributions grow tax-deferred. The plans also permit employers to make tax-deductible matching contributions to each employee's account so long as they meet the nondiscrimination tests of the Internal Revenue Code. Workers can elect to make pretax contributions through salary reduction agreements, sometimes matched by employers, in "savings" accounts managed by the employer. The taxes become due and payable when the funds are withdrawn. Regulations finalized in 1991 caused employers to lose the ability to restructure their 401(k)s after 1991 to help higher-paid employees obtain maximum deferrals. However, employers will be able to make hardship withdrawals easier for financially distressed participants. *See also* money-purchase pension plan.

secular trust Similar to the popular **rabbi trust**. A relatively new executive perk that provides taxable supplementary pension benefits for corporate executives.

self-designed pay plan A form of executive incentive plan that allows participants to choose the form in which their incentive payments are to be made. Sometimes called a *cafeteria plan*. *See also* bonus payment; book value plan; market value plan; stock options.

self-funded plan of benefits A plan in which the employer provides an indemnity type plan to employees on a self-funded basis (not through an insurance company) and purchases stop-loss coverage from a reinsurer to reimburse the self-funded plan when claims exceed a set amount (usually $20,000) for any one individual. Typically such a plan also has an aggregate stop loss, which establishes that if claims exceed a set amount, such as $200,000, on all employees and dependents, the reinsurance carrier would also reimburse the self-funded plan for the excess aggregate amount.

self-insurance group (SIG) An alternative means of obtaining insurance coverage for workers' compensation claims in which employers band together to finance exposure to insurance risk and, at the same time, earn investment income on the funds.

self-insured benefits plan (SIBP) A benefits plan administered and supported in its entirety by the organization rather than by insurance carriers.

self-managed account (SMA) Allowing employees to choose from among such investments as mutual funds, fixed-income securities, and stocks listed on domestic exchanges when creating their investment portfolios, with the intention of making them satisfied with their 401(k) plan.

semi-bundled services Investment services offered employees by organizations that permit workers to choose a combination of in-house and outside sources, including those offered by independent outside sources. *See also* bundled services; unbundled services.

sexual harassment 1. Defined by the Equal Employment Opportunity Commission as "unwelcome sexual advances, requests for sexual favors, and other verbal (such as telling sexual jokes) or physical conduct (pinching, putting arms around a person, or touching) of a sexual nature . . . when such submission to or rejection of this conduct explicitly or implicitly affects an individual's employment, unreasonably interferes with an individual's work performance or creates an intimidating, hostile, or offensive work environment." **2.** A form of discrimination resulting from different treatment of the sexes, such as unwanted overt or subtle sexual overtures leading to differential job-related outcomes. Unlawful sex discrimination may take either of two forms: (1) *Quid pro quo* harassment, which occurs when a supervisor conditions the granting of an economic benefit, such as promotion, upon the receipt of sexual favors from a subordinate or punishes the subordinate for refusing to submit to his or her request (termination, loss of salary increases, or demotion), or (2) *hostile work environment* harassment, which occurs where supervisors or co-workers create an atmosphere so infused with unwelcome sexually oriented conduct that an individual's reasonable comfort or ability to perform his or her job is affected. Examples of the latter include intimidation, hostility, physical contact, suggestive comments, off-color jokes, and pressure for dates. *See also* Interpretative Guidelines on Sexual Harassment.

sheddable worker One that is a part of a force of contingent workers hired to supplement a core group of full-time employees that operate the business from day to day—a worker that can be laid off when not needed. Also called *assignment worker, contingent worker, disposable worker, flexible worker,* and *throwaway worker. See also* contingent work force.

short-term income protection State-administered and, with a few exceptions, entirely employer-financed programs designed to protect workers during periods of joblessness.

short-time compensation The use of partial payments from unemployment insurance systems for workers whose salaries have been reduced to support continued employment rather than waiting until workers have been laid off. The practice has been facilitated by legislation in Arizona, Arkansas, California, Florida, Kansas, Louisiana, Maryland, Massachusetts, Missouri, New York, Oregon, Texas, Vermont, and Washington.

significant activities of daily living (SADLs) In the health care field, to qualify for benefits under a long-term care insurance policy, the insured must be totally dependent on human assistance in performing a specific number (usually three) of the following significant activities of daily living: bathing, eating, dressing, toileting, transferring from bed to chair, and maintaining continence.

significant other Attributed to Harry Stack Sullivan, noted psychiatrist. Describes a spouse, sweetheart, lover, partner, parent, child, grandparent, daughter/son-in-law, friend, or companion; an individual who has an important impact on one's welfare, happiness, or emotional security. *See also* domestic partner.

simplified employee pension (SEP) A group of individual retirement accounts (IRAs) established by employees but funded by the employer. Such plans are limited to closely held companies or sole proprietorships. Contributions are flexible; the employer decides how much to contribute, depending on business conditions, up to a limit of 15 percent of gross compensation or $30,000, whichever is less. Contributions are tax-deductible and grow tax-deferred as long as they remain in the SEP-IRA. Self-employed persons may contribute up to 13.04 percent of net earnings. Employees control their own accounts and are fully vested at all times.

Single Employer Pension Plan Amendments Act of 1986 (SEPPA) Included in the **Consolidated Omnibus Budget Reconciliation Act of 1986**. Revised funding requirements for pension plans.

single-payer plan An advanced form of universal health care plan, similar to Canada's health care system, in which the federal government would eliminate Medicare, Medicaid, and employer-funded insurance, replace private insurers, underwrite the coverage, and negotiate physicians' fees. *See also* managed competition plan.

skill-based pay A nontraditional form of compensation; pay for what employees can do regardless of their positions or length of service with the organization.

skunk works A term borrowed from the "L'il Abner" comic strip and applied to business by the Lockheed California Company, where it is called Skunk Works, a registered service mark. The term was also used by Tom Peters and Nancy Austin (Foreword to *A Passion for Excellence*, New York, Random House, 1984). It refers to a creative, innovative, fast-paced, and somewhat unconventional undertaking operating at the periphery of the organization.

smile sheet A trainee reaction form. A common approach to the evaluation of training in which trainees are asked for their opinions about the value of the course, seminar, or workshop, the instructor, and the training setting.

smile training A cynical term recently applied to customer-service training that focuses on developing people who can act friendly toward customers by teaching nonverbal behaviors that convey friendliness.

Social Security Act of 1935 (SSA) Legislation that created and implemented a worker-employer-government insurance program covering retirement, survivors, disability, and **Medicare** benefits. In 1993 individuals pay 6.2 percent on earnings up to $57,600 through withholding. That amount is matched dollar for dollar by the employer and sent to the Social Security Administration. Medicare tax for 1993 is 1.45 percent on income up to $135,000. Retirement benefits begin at age 65 (full benefits) or 62 (reduced benefits). The amount people can earn annually in 1993 (earnings test) without losing Social Security benefits is $10,560 for people age 65 through 69, and for every $3 earned over the exemption amount, $1 in Social Security benefits is withheld. For those younger than 65, the exemption is $7,680, and for every $2 earned over the exemption amount, $1 in Social Security benefits is withheld. The earnings test does not apply for people over 70. Beginning in 2003, the age for full retirement will be raised to 65 years and two months; by 2027, the age will be 67. Other benefits include **Supplemental Security Income**, unemployment insurance, food stamps, child support enforcement, family and child welfare services, workers' compensation, veterans' benefits, help for the blind, and several other special programs. Some are cooperative programs with state governments; many are administered by state public-assistance offices. *See also* Federal Insurance Contributions Act of 1935.

Soldiers' and Sailors' Civil Relief Act of 1991 Amended the Soldiers' and Sailors' Civil Relief Act of 1940 to clarify veterans' reemployment rights and improve veterans' rights to reinstatement of health insurance based on assessments of need for supportive services, skills, and talents.

staff leasing Used originally by small businesses and professional practices to minimize the cost of providing benefits to lower-skilled employees, leased staff are now employed to save time and costs, provide professional skills unavailable within the company, and reduce turnover. Staff leasing differs from temporary employees in that leased staff are hired by the employing company, stay on the job for an indefinite period of time, and enjoy portable benefits, while temporary employees are recruited by the temp agency, remain on the job for a limited period of time, and lack comprehensive benefits.

staff model health maintenance organization (SMHMO) An HMO that owns and operates health care centers staffed by physicians employed directly by the HMO. Centers may provide laboratory, X-ray, drug and alcohol treatment programs, prescription drugs, and other medical services. Affiliated hospitals provide inpatient services to members. *See also* group practice health maintenance organization.

standard hour plan Similar to a piecework incentive plan, the standard hour plan rewards workers by granting a percent premium above the base rate that equals the percent by which their performance exceeds the prescribed standard.

standards of care Standards that describe circumstances under which certain medical or surgical procedures should and should not be performed. They are developed and refined by expert physicians through review of published research and personal experience.

state employment postings Mandatory employment postings required by all 50 states, although requirements differ from state to state. Most states require fair employment law, minimum wage, state occupational safety and health, and workers' compensation posters. *See also* labor law posting.

Statement No. 95, FASB Issued by the Financial Accounting Standards Board in November 1987, Statement No. 95 requires public companies to replace the standard Statement of Changes in Financial Position with a Statement of Cash Flows in financial reports.

statutory benefits Benefits mandated by federal and state laws. They include social security (FICA), workers' compensation, and unemployment compensation. Sometimes partly supported by employee contributions. *See also* benefits; entitlements; protection benefits.

stock appreciation rights plan (SAR) An executive compensation plan that allows for the payment of undetermined amounts tied to the dividend record of the company or to the gain in the company's stock price over a specified period of time without the actual purchase of stock by the participant. Employees are credited with a number of stock units without ownership rights in the stock itself. *See also* performance achievement plan; restricted stock plan.

stock equivalent plan A form of long-term incentive plan. Includes **book value plans, phantom stock plans,** and **dividend equivalent plans**.

stock options Financial incentives to improve effort and productivity, usually directed toward managerial, scientific, and technical employees. Employees are given the right to purchase a specified amount of stock at a certain price for a stated period of time when they have qualified for such a reward. Options prices are usually considerably lower than the prevailing market prices, and the difference between the option and the market price is the value of the option at any given time. Include incentive stock options, nonqualified stock options, and stock appreciation rights. *See also* market value plan; self-designed pay plan; performance achievement plan.

stop loss 1. A provision in health or disability insurance policies that places a ceiling on the amount the employee has to pay (the deductible) as his or her share of a claim. **2.** A provision that limits aggregate losses in self-funded health or disability plans to a specific agreed-upon annual amount. The carrier pays the employer (policyholder) for claims in excess of the agreed-upon amount.

structured settlement An alternative to insurance lump sum settlement. A financial arrangement that allows the defendant in a lawsuit to pay off today's claims with tomorrow's dollars—clearing the books of everything from $3,000 personal injury claims through million-dollar malpractice claims to multimillion-dollar class action suits—by stretching out payments over a period of 5, 10, or 20 years, or a lifetime. Typically, the defendant buys an annuity from a life insurance company (or the annuity is self-funded by a corporation or institution) that makes payments to the injured party over several years. The defendant also gets a fast settlement and reduced settlement costs. The plaintiff receives tax- and worry-free guaranteed income tailored to his or her needs over the payment period.

substitution of benefits or employee stock option (ownership) plan (ESOP) benefits A plan for meeting retiree medical liabilities in which benefits are funded by reducing the benefits of the retiree medical plan and compensating employees with other increased benefits such as pensions or ESOPs.

summary annual report (SAR) A summary of key financial information taken from annual **Form 5500 filings** about a company's retirement plan as required by federal law. Copies of the SAR must be distributed to all plan participants. *See also* ERISA bond; summary plan description.

summary jury trial An **alternative dispute resolution procedure** in which the parties to the controversy agree to employ a mock six-member jury, empaneled by a court, to render a nonbinding verdict on the dispute. The purpose of the procedure is to demonstrate to the parties how a jury might decide the case. *See also* arbitration; fact-finding, med-arb; mediation; mini-trial; rent-a-judge.

summary plan description (SPD) A written description of a company's benefit plan. An SPD is an important part of a plan to communicate benefits information to employees and is required by the **Employee Retirement Income Security Act of 1974**. SPDs should be specific, simple, complete, and written in plain English. *See also* ERISA bond; Form 5500 filings; summary annual report.

summative evaluation An approach to the evaluation of training systems that focuses on the effectiveness of the program in terms of the results obtained as compared with the resources expended. *See also* formative evaluation.

Superfund Amendments and Reauthorization Act of 1986 (SARA) An act relating to health and physical hazards of chemicals in the workplace and hazardous waste operations. It significantly revised, expanded, and extended the provisions of the **Comprehensive Environmental Response, Compensation, and Liability Act of 1980,**

commonly known as the Superfund Law. *See also* Hazard Communication Standard of 1988.

supplemental executive retirement plan (SERP) A tailored financial arrangement that functions as a retirement plan for key employees where there is no qualified retirement plan. SERPs help retain key executives, make compensation packages more competitive, help with necessary or desirable early retirement, protect benefits in a merger situation, and restore benefits stripped from higher-paid executives by recent changes in tax laws. Sometimes called a *salary continuation plan*.

supplemental pay benefits Benefits paid for time not worked. They include unemployment insurance, vacation and holiday pay, sick pay, bereavement pay, severance pay, and **supplemental unemployment benefits**.

supplemental protection plan Benefits designed to afford additional protection to workers while they are employed and after retirement. Examples are death, disability, and medical insurance policies that provide higher amounts of coverage than the group plan in effect and, mainly for executives, equity-based plans funded by the company that provide postretirement income and equity.

Supplemental Security Income (SSI) A joint federal and state program for low-income persons that has no premiums and deductibles. It pays monthly checks to people who are 65 or older, who are blind, or who have a disability and have little or no property or income. Disabled and blind children are also eligible for monthly checks. People who receive SSI are usually eligible for the Food Stamp Program and Medicaid as well. Basic SSI payments are the same nationwide; however, many states add money to the basic check.

supplemental unemployment benefits (SUB) Supplements to state unemployment insurance payments funded and paid by employers to unemployed workers. They are typically paid during periods of layoff, reduced workweeks, and relocation. *See also* guaranteed annual income.

survivors' benefits Lump-sum or monthly payments made by an organization to the surviving spouse or children of an employee or annuitant. In addition to private corporations, survivors' benefits are also paid by federal and state governments (Social Security and armed forces annuitants, for example). Invariably, maximum payments are established and age limits are set for the surviving spouse and dependent children.

sweetheart deal Preferential treatment afforded to individuals or groups in such areas as contracts, perquisites, compensation (raises and bonuses) and benefits (retirement).

T

TA	**1.** Task analysis. **2.** Transportation Act of 1989.
TAMRA	Technical Corrections and Miscellaneous Revenue Act of 1988.
TAW	Train America's Workforce.
TBP	Target benefit plan.
TDUR	Therapeutic drug utilization review.
TERA	Tax Equity and Responsibility Act of 1982.
TPA	Third-party administrator.
TPS	Tiered premium system.
TRA	Tax Reform Act of 1986.
TSA	Tax-sheltered annuity.
TSP	Thrift Savings Plan.
TTTA	Training Technology Transfer Act of 1984.

Taft-Hartley Act *See* Labor-Management Relations Act of 1947.

Taft-Hartley Amendment of 1990 Legislation that allows unions to negotiate for housing assistance for their members. In addition to earlier anticorruption provisions prohibiting management from making direct payments to unions except for certain purposes such as employee education, health care, and retirement, the Amendment adds housing to the list of exemptions. *See also* Labor-Management Relations Act of 1947.

target benefit plan (TBP) A hybrid type of **defined contribution plan** in which contributions are determined as though the plan were a **defined benefit plan;** however, the amount of benefit received at retirement depends on the value of the assets in the worker's account, just as it does in a defined contribution plan.

task A level in the structure of work. One of the work operations that is a logical and essential step in the performance of a duty. That is, every duty is made up of one or more tasks, and a task has the same relationship to a duty as a duty has to a job. A task is a work unit that defines and describes the methods, procedure, and techniques by which a duty is carried out. Each task has these characteristics: It is performed in a relatively short period of time (seconds, minutes, or hours but rarely days or longer); it occurs with reasonable frequency in the work cycle; it is an independent and finite part of a duty; it is performed by one person (not shared or divided with another worker); it involves closely related skills, knowledge, and abilities; and it is performed in accordance with some standard. For example, an electronic equipment repairer's servicing duty might include cleaning, lubricating, replacing tubes, and filling reservoirs with hydraulic fluid. *See also* duty; element; job.

task analysis (TA) The lowest practicable level of analysis; the process of defining the behaviors, conditions, and standards of a task and identifying the elements that distinguish that task from other tasks. *See also* job analysis.

Tax Equity and Responsibility Act of 1982 (TERA) Legislation that made Medicare the secondary insurer and employer-provided plans the primary insurance source for active employees aged 65 to 69. The law has since been amended to include working spouses younger than age 65 and active employees older than 69.

Tax Reform Act of 1986 (TRA) Established nondiscrimination standards for employee compensation and benefits, limited certain salary deferral plans, and set new standards for pretax benefit plans, loans, and pensions. The Act greatly reduced the usefulness of IRAs by restricting the tax deductibility of contributions, based on adjusted gross income for active participants in company pension plans. IRS regulations that became effective January 1, 1991, provide guidance on the retirement plan nondiscrimination rules added or changed by the Act. Among other things, the regulations were designed to simplify the previously proposed minimum participation requirements under Section 401(a)(26) and provide new tests to ensure that benefits plans do not discriminate in favor of highly compensated workers. *See also* Deficit Reduction Act of 1984.

tax-sheltered annuity (TSA) Provides retirement income for workers of certain tax-exempt organizations. Amounts saved can accumulate tax-free and sometimes provide other tax advantages; however, amounts paid to annuitants at retirement are treated as ordinary income and so taxed. The **Tax Reform Act of 1986** modified the amount that may be contributed to TSAs. Also referred to as *tax-deferred annuity*.

Technical Corrections and Miscellaneous Revenue Act of 1988 (TAMRA) The Act requires employers to report the total amount of dependent care assistance provided for each employee.

telecommuting center A modification of work-at-home programs. Instead of traveling to their normal offices, workers drive to a center established within their area containing workstations, phone lines, modems, fax machines, and copiers. The arrangement cuts commute time and eliminates the interruptions workers might encounter at home.

temporary employees Corporate executives, managers, technicians, physicians, nurses, pharmacists, accountants, or office workers hired on a temporary basis to meet seasonal or emergency requirements, which cannot be met through organizational resources. Provides a means of remaining globally competitive and avoiding the ups and downs of market cycles and the growing burdens of employment rules, antidiscrimination laws, health care costs, and pension plans. Also called *contingent workers, disposable workers, extra workers, just-in-time employees, peripherals,* and *temps. See also* core workers.

termination-at-will The traditional rule that where there is no contract, the employment relationship can be terminated "at will" (for any reason or no reason) by either the employer or the employee. That rule has been superseded due to litigation. *See also* employment-at-will; retaliatory discharge.

test security **1.** The right of a testee to privacy of information relating to test results and the right to informed consent about the use of those results. **2.** The right of a testee to expect that no one taking the test has access to the test or information about its contents that would give him or her unfair advantage over other test takers.

therapeutic drug utilization review (TDUR) Programs designed to reduce costs by identifying inappropriate or overly costly prescribing patterns of therapy regimens within an employee prescription drug plan. Studies typically target high-dollar-volume therapeutic categories, such as antiulcer, antiarthritis, and cardiovascular medications. *See also* drug formulary; drug utilization review.

third party administrator (TPA) A company that handles Medicare and other health care insurance claims and utilization review for the federal government or corporations. TPAs may offer precertification, a second opinion program, and catastrophic case management. Essentially the job of TPAs is to settle claims problems. They also provide a means of reducing costs by providing outside experts to monitor, evaluate, and control health care services.

thrift savings plan (TSP) A form of equity benefit, a thrift savings plan serves as an adjunct or supplement to noncontributory pension plans. Employees are given the option of saving through payroll deductions a designated percentage of their regular pay in one or more available investment opportunities, usually matched dollar for dollar by the employer. *See also* capital accumulation plan; defined contribution plan.

tiered benefits plan A cost savings device that expands employees' eligibility for benefits over a specified period of time rather than granting full benefits immediately upon employment.

tiered premium system (TPS) A health care cost-cutting strategy in which premiums for coverage are established at different rates for employee only, employee and spouse, and employee, spouse, and children.

tin parachute A novel type of severance plan designed to protect employees when company ownership changes. A variant of the **golden parachute**, which guarantees hefty payments to key executives in the event of takeovers or mergers, tin parachutes assure lower-level employees of similar benefits. For example, some plans entitle all employees to cash payments of up to two and one-half times their annual compensation, including bonuses and incentive pay, if company ownership changes as a consequence of a hostile takeover. Because of the number of employees they apply to, the plans serve as a deterrent to raiders by making takeovers prohibitively expensive. *See also* bronze parachute.

Title VII Title VII of the **Civil Rights Act of 1964**, amended in 1972, which prohibits employment practices that discriminate on the bases of sex, race, color, religion, or national origin. With later Executive Orders, it requires employers of more than 100 workers to file annual equal employment opportunity reports with the Equal Employment Opportunity Commission. *See also* discrimination; disparate impact; fetal protection policy; fetal risk; protected characteristics; protected class; religious accommodation.

Train America's Workforce (TAW) A campaign initiated and sponsored by the American Society for Training and Development. Its purpose is to encourage and promote the additional training that American workers (executives and managers, technicians, customer service workers, and other employees) will need over the next decade to keep up with the changes demanded by their jobs. TAW will cover all 50 states. For further information call the TAW hotline, 703/683-9599.

training Formal or informal, group or individual short-term learning experiences designed to impart or improve the skills, knowledge, and job performance of employees, franchisees, dealers, or clients. Its immediate goal is new job skills or improved competency—the ability to do something or do it better. It takes place *before* it is needed. *See also* development; education.

Training Technology Transfer Act of 1984 (TTTA) Established the Office of Training Technology Transfer to facilitate the transfer of training technology from the agencies of the federal government, including the Department of Defense, to the private sector and state and local governments with special attention to the requirements of small business.

transitional employment Providing alternative work for a limited time that will be useful to the organization and, at the same time, serve as rehabilitative assignments for employees who have been absent due to illness or injury. Rather than paying disability benefits, the organization brings workers back to the workplace as soon as medical providers approve of the return and places them in temporary modified-duty, light-duty, or restructured jobs until they are sufficiently recovered to return to their original positions.

Transportation Act of 1989 (TA) A bill that includes mandatory drug and alcohol testing of transportation workers. Specifically, the bill calls for random, preemployment, postaccident, and for-cause testing of employees in safety-sensitive positions in the airline, rail, bus, and trucking industries. *See also* drug testing.

triple option point-of-service health care plan A managed care model. Gives enrollees three options at the point where they need health care: (1) going through their primary care physician (least expensive); (2) going directly to another network; or (3) going outside of the network (highest deductibles and copayments).

tuition-aid program A formal corporate program and plan that provides financial assistance to employees who take credit or noncredit courses from accredited schools and colleges on their own time. In some cases financial backing is provided only for training and education programs that are directly related to the employee's current job. In other organizations, tuition aid is granted for high school equivalency courses, general postsecondary education programs and cultural courses, and advanced degree programs for employees—and sometimes for the employee's spouse or children. *See also* institutional partnerships.

turkey trot The practice of transferring a marginal, incompetent, or problem employee from one department or job to another in the hope that a new environment and a new boss will give the person a fresh start.

two-tier pay structure A compensation plan that brings new hires into the work force of an organization at a lower rate of pay (as much as 50 percent lower) than was given to employees hired earlier for similar jobs.

U

UCR   Usual, customary, and reasonable.
ULPs   Unfair labor practices.
UM   Utilization management.
UR   Utilization review.

ultimate evaluation Examination and assessment of the changes in the results achieved by organizations, departments, managers, supervisors, or employees when they have experienced or been subjected to some organization development or training and development intervention. Measures used focus on such outcomes as increased productivity, improved quality of products or services, and reduced operating costs. Examples are decreases or reductions in absenteeism, accident rates, customer complaints, grievances, labor disputes, machine damage and downtime, operating costs, rejects and reworks, and turnover; and increases or improvements in attendance, customer satisfaction, new processes, new products, product quality and quantity, profit and return on investment, and sales. *See also* external evaluation; immediate evaluation; intermediate evaluation.

unbundled services Options offered employees that permit workers to choose whatever investment alternatives they would like, including those offered by independent outside sources such as national full-service 401(k) vendors. *See also* bundled services; semi-bundled services.

underutilization In affirmative action, when determining the status of minority group employment in a company by geographic area, department, and job, the finding that members of protected groups are not adequately represented or that there is a concentration of nonminority workers. Analysis of data provides a basis for remedies in the form of affirmative action programs.

undue burden or hardship Under the **Americans with Disabilities Act**

154

of 1990, the term means an action requiring significant difficulty of expense to a business to make "**reasonable accommodation**" to the disability of a qualified applicant or employee. Factors included for consideration in determining if a reasonable accommodation actually constitutes an "undue hardship" include the nature and cost of the accommodation, the financial resources of the employer, and the impact of the accommodation on the financial resources of the employer. "Undue burden" is a higher standard than "readily achievable."

unemployment compensation A form of statutory benefit. State laws or regulations provide that employees who are involuntarily unemployed may receive compensation in stated amounts and for a stipulated period of time unless they are able to secure gainful employment. Programs are funded by payroll taxes levied entirely upon employers (except in Alabama, Alaska, New Jersey, and Pennsylvania, where employees are required to make small contributions), although they are sometimes supplemented by federal funds (usually during periods of severe and general high unemployment), and administered by the states.

Unemployment Compensation Amendments Act of 1992 Extended emergency unemployment benefits programs for long-term jobless workers who had exhausted their regular 26 weeks of benefits. Included a provision designed to pay for the increased unemployment benefits involving a change in qualified plan distribution and rollover rules. The law requires that all qualified retirement plans permit rollover of any taxable portion of a distribution from another qualified plan or tax-sheltered annuity, unless it is a minimum required distribution or part of a series of long-term payments. Qualified plans making distributions must permit their distributions to be rolled over into an **individual retirement account** or another plan specified by the plan participant. If the plan participant does not specify a rollover into another plan or IRA, the employer plan making the distribution must withhold 20 percent of the distribution in addition to any penalties for early withdrawal that apply. Signed by President Bush July 3, 1992, and became effective December 31, 1992.

unfair labor practices (ULPs) 1. As defined by the **Wagner Act of 1935**, such employer practices as (1) interfering with, restraining, or coercing employees in exercising their legally sanctioned right of self-organization; (2) dominating or interfering with either the formation or administration of labor unions, including bribery of employees, company spy systems, moving a business to avoid unionization, and blacklisting union sympathizers; (3) discriminating in any way against employees for their legal union activities; (4) discharging or discriminating against employees because they have filed unfair practice charges against the company; and (5) refusing to bargain collectively with their employees' representatives. **2.** As defined by the **Labor-Management Relations Act of 1947** (Taft-Hartley), union practices such as (1) restraining or coercing employees from exercising their guaranteed bargaining rights; (2) causing an employer to discriminate in any way against an employee in order to encourage or discourage membership in a union; (3) refusing to bargain "in good faith" with the employer about wages, hours, and other employment conditions (and certain types of strikes and boycotts); and (4) engaging in "featherbedding" (requiring an employer to pay for services not performed).

unfairly discriminatory Any policy or action that results in unequal probabilities of selection for training, hiring, or other favorable outcome for persons (members of a minority group or women) who have equal probabilities of success (with nonminorities) in the job or training program.

uniform coverage rule An Internal Revenue Service rule. States that plan participants who elect health care flexible spending accounts (FSAs) must be afforded uniform coverage throughout the coverage period, just as with other medical plans. Employers may not withhold FSA claims reimbursements until the FSA balance of employee pretax contributions justifies the reimbursement. Instead, employers must make reimbursements for qualified FSA claims at all times during a year on the basis of the total amount of annual contributions made by the employee during enrollment.

Uniform Guidelines on Employee Selection Procedures Approved in 1978 by the Equal Employment Opportunity Commission, Civil Service Commission, Department of Labor, and Department of Justice, and published by the Equal Employment Opportunity Commission. Contain "highly recommended" procedures for such things as employee selection, record keeping, preemployment inquiries, and affirmative action programs. *See also Griggs* v. *Duke Power.*

unionization The establishment of collective bargaining between an employer and the work force as a unit.

union shop An accommodation or arrangement with a union where the firm can hire nonunion employees but they must join the union after a prescribed period of time and pay dues; it they don't, they can be fired. *See also* agency shop; closed shop; maintenance of membership; open shop.

universal health care plan A plan by which the federal government would draw up a catalog of minimum health care benefits for all

Americans. Private companies would continue to offer coverage to workers under employer-funded plans and develop policies to cover the costs of experimental or high-risk procedures. *See also* single-payer plan.

universal precautions Mandatory regulations issued by the Department of Labor's Occupational Safety and Health Administration in December 1991 that became effective in March 1992. Designed to protect workers, primarily but not exclusively health care providers, from health risks associated with their work. The regulations cover all health care facilities, including hospitals, clinics, hospices, nursing homes, and doctors' and dentists' offices. They also cover other occupations in which workers may be exposed to contaminated substances, such as funeral homes, emergency teams, law enforcement units, correctional facilities, linen services, and medical equipment repair companies. Employers are required to provide, at their own expense, voluntary inoculations for their employees to prevent hepatitis B. The regulations also require employers to institute engineering controls, such as puncture-resistant containers for used needles, and protective equipment, such as impermeable gowns, gloves, and face masks, and the enforcement of work practices to reduce infections, such as hand-washing. The standard also requires appropriate labeling and training to alert workers to the risks posed by bloodborne organisms. Facilities that use concentrated viruses are required to post warning signs. Employers are required to keep records of incidents of exposure, postexposure follow-up, hepatitis B vaccinations, and employee training.

unsafe acts Such causes of accidents and injuries as distractions (horseplay or startling), failing to secure equipment or tools, failing to wear safe clothing or use protective equipment, lifting improperly, making safety devices inoperative (removing or disconnecting them), operating or working at unsafe speed (either too fast or too slowly), throwing objects or materials, using unsafe equipment or tools, using equipment or tools unsafely, using unsafe procedures in arranging, loading, placing, combining, or mixing, and taking unsafe positions under suspended loads. *See also* unsafe conditions.

unsafe conditions Such hazards as defective equipment and tools, hazardous arrangement or congestion of machines or equipment, hazardous procedures in using equipment and tools, improperly guarded equipment and tools, improper illumination, inadequate ventilation or impure air sources, overloading, and unsafe storage. *See also* unsafe acts.

uptraining Training designed to improve employees' performance of current skills and teach new skills. Sometimes called *redeployment.* Includes **cross-training.**

upward mobility 1. Readiness of employees to assume more responsible or more demanding positions. Refers primarily to the preparation and promotion of minorities into more demanding and remunerative jobs, including managerial positions. **2.** Programs designed to identify specific jobs as targets for underdeveloped employees, advertise projected vacancies in those jobs, identify and advertise bridge positions leading to the target jobs, identify specific qualifications for each job, restrict competition for bridge and upward mobility jobs to underemployed, underdeveloped, and underutilized employees and applicants, prepare individual development plans for selected individuals, and identify and implement specific training and development activities for each upward mobility position. *See also* affirmative action.

use it or lose it rule An Internal Revenue Service rule that prohibits income deferrals (of benefits) throughout the implementation of cafeteria plans. For example, unused flexible spending account credits from the current year plan may not be saved or deferred into a later plan year. If no other option is selected, they are paid to the employee as fully taxable income. Similarly, elective vacation purchases must be used in the year purchased or they are forfeited.

usual, customary, and reasonable (UCR) In its abbreviated form, used by insurance companies in connection with setting base fees. UCR means that payment will be made for charges the subscriber is legally responsible to pay based on the normal, fair, and established charge for a covered service or treatment (the same or similar) in the same service area.

utilization management (UM) Management of health care programs to control costs. Involves data analysis of claims, identification of specific utilization problems, evaluation of benefits to ensure that employees have incentives to use alternative less costly treatment settings, and, based on findings, revise benefits packages.

utilization review (UR) A common part of employees' health benefits packages. Involves a focused review of the use of the benefits over time. UR seeks to identify specific problems relating to variations in practice among specific categories, such as providers, facilities, or geographic areas, and the severity of illnesses, through sophisticated data analysis. Following review and analysis of the problems, **utilization management** programs are used to address the problems, the program is implemented, results are audited and measured, and information is fed back to the provider.

V

VEVRA   Vietnam Era Veterans Readjustment and Assistance Act of 1974.

VRBA   Veterans' Readjustment Benefits Act of 1966.

validity An essential characteristic of tests, ratings, and other psychological measures. Indicates the extent to which the instrument measures what it was supposed to measure and that scores or ratings provided by the instrument predict or correlate significantly with important aspects of job performance. *See also* reliability.

variable annuity An annuity or pension in which the amount paid to retirees varies according to the investment yield of the funds set aside to provide it. *See also* group annuity.

variable compensation Any kind of pay given strictly on the basis of employee or organizational performance; a reward for outstanding performance. Options include special cash awards, special performance targets, lump-sum merit, profit-sharing, team incentives, and gain sharing.

vendor program In benefits, an employer-sponsored dependent care option in which an employer subsidizes dependent care slots in group day care centers or family day care homes.

vested or vesting 1. A benefits plan provision that entitles employees to all or a portion of accrued benefits in company pension plans even if they are placed on long-term or permanent layoff prior to retirement. The **Employee Retirement Income Security Act of 1974** specifies the standards for vesting of employee contributions and is made more restrictive by the Tax Reform Act of 1986. **2.** That point in time when an executive can exercise stock option or **stock appreciation rights** or some other executive compensation plan can no longer be forfeited.

Veterans' Readjustment Benefits Act of 1966 (VRBA) As amended by the Vietnam Era Veterans Readjustment Assistance Act of 1974 (P.L.

93-508) and by P.L. 100-212 of 1988. An act designed to meet the special employment and training needs of disabled veterans and Vietnam-era veterans and increase their opportunities to obtain employment, job training, counseling, and job placement services.

viatical settlement A form of living benefit by which companies (not insurance carriers), backed by private investors and pension and corporate funds, purchase life insurance policies for between 15 and 95 percent of their face value in exchange for being named the beneficiary. The shorter the individual's life expectancy, the higher the percentage paid. People with huge medical bills and short life expectancies sell their policies to get immediate cash; companies purchase the policies to get a quick return on investment. Considered unconscionable, even ghoulish, by some, but realistic and defensible by others. *See also* living benefits.

Vietnam Era Veterans Readjustment and Assistance Act of 1974 (VEVRA) Legislation passed by Congress to promote the hiring of "qualified disabled veterans" and "veterans of the Vietnam era." The Act proscribes discrimination against those veterans and requires affirmative action to hire and promote them. Qualified disabled veterans are those who receive disability compensation for a 30 percent or greater disability or who were discharged or released from active duty for an injury received or aggravated in the line of duty. Veterans of the Vietnam era are individuals who were on active duty more than 180 days between August 5, 1964, and May 5, 1975, and were not dishonorably discharged, or were on active duty between those dates and were released for a service-connected disability. The Act applies only to federal contractors and subcontractors with contracts of $10,000 or more. Larger contractors (with contracts worth $50,000 or more and 50 or more employees) must also prepare affirmative action programs.

vision care plan A form of protection benefit, a plan by which reimbursements are provided to covered employees for limited optometric examinations and lens prescriptions.

voluntary bargaining item In union contract negotiations, an item over which bargaining is neither required (mandatory) nor prohibited (unlawful), and neither party can be compelled to negotiate. *See also* mandatory bargaining item.

voucher program An employer-sponsored and -financed dependent care option in which the employee submits monthly vouchers for dependent care expenses to the provider and the employer covers all or a part of the cost of the services. *See also* dependent care assistance plan.

W

wage curve Used to assign pay rates to pay grades (jobs of approximately equal difficulty that have been grouped together). Wage curves depict graphically the pay rates currently being paid for jobs in each pay grade relative to the points or rankings awarded to each job or grade during job evaluation. *See also* compensable factors; job evaluation.

wage gap The difference between men's and women's pay for the same or comparable work. *See also* comparable worth.

wage structure Graphically depicts the range of pay rates (such as dollars and cents per hour) to be paid each pay grade in a series of jobs. Derived from the **wage curve**, but additional information, such as market wages, compensation policies, and required rate changes are taken into account to produce the final wage structure—the wages to be paid by the company categorized by pay grades and indicating rate changes.

Wagner Act of 1935 (WA) *See* National Labor Relations Act of 1935; unfair labor practices.

Walsh-Healy Public Contracts Act of 1936 (WHPCA) An act that established basic labor standards for such items as minimum (prevailing) wage rates, overtime, health and safety requirements, and fringe benefits. The Act also establishes liability for breaches of contract for the manufacture or furnishing of materials, supplies, articles, and equipment. It applies to organizations working on federal government contracts of $10,000 or more.

Weingarten Rule (or Rights) Interprets the **National Labor Relations Act of 1935** in relation to unfair labor practices and the questioning of employees by employers. States that an employer violates the NLRA by requiring an employee to take part in an investigatory interview without union representation if the employee requests representation. However, an employer may refuse to bargain with any union representative permitted to attend an interview. An employee is not entitled to representation at a meeting with management where management has already decided in advance of the meeting to terminate the employee and the sole purpose of the meeting is to inform the employee of that fact. *See also* Anti-Injunction Act of 1932; employee rights.

whipsawing A term used by labor to describe the practice of forcing plant-against-plant competition or bidding for jobs. The threat of closings, whether specifically made or only implied, is used as a lever to gain approval of cost-saving measures unless unions make concessions with respect to such items as compensation, benefits, scheduling, or work rules.

Whistleblower Protection Act of 1989 (WPA) An act designed to protect the rights of federal employees who make disclosures of illegality, corruption, fraud, waste, abuse, and unnecessary government expenditures, prevent reprisals, and help eliminate wrongdoing within the government. The Act established the Office of Special Counsel to receive and investigate allegations of prohibited personnel practices, bring petitions for corrective actions, file complaints or make recommendations for disciplinary action, and, where appropriate, forward to the Attorney General or an agency head disclosures of violations of any law, rule, or regulation, gross mismanagement, waste of funds, abuse of authority, or substantial and specific danger to public health or safety. *See also* False Claims Act Amendment of 1986.

Williams-Steiger Act of 1970 (WSA) *See* Occupational Safety and Health Act of 1970 (OSHA).

work and family programs Work accommodations and benefits programs designed to help equalize benefits, serve as recruiting and retention incentives, and build goodwill among employees. Examples are adoption assistance program, dependent care assistance plan, employee home ownership plan, family care program, flexible leave, **flexiplace**, home leave, home marketing assistance, home sales protection, **job sharing/job splitting**, maternity and child care, and parental leave.

work distribution chart A device used to improve work flow, allocate time to work processes, distribute work evenly, and reduce employee boredom or fatigue. The chart is developed by determining what tasks are being performed in a work area, who by name is doing them, and how much time is spent on each one. The chart is analyzed by a knowledgeable supervisor to improve task assignment and performance. *See also* work measurement.

Worker Adjustment and Retraining Notification Act of 1988 (WARNA) An act requiring that as of February 4, 1989, workers in companies with 100 or more full-time employees receive a minimum of 60 days' written advance notice in the event of a massive layoff or plant closing involving 50 or more people. The law allows employers to provide less than 60 days' notice when they are seeking new customers, trying to raise capital or when the closures or layoffs are due to unforeseen conditions or natural disasters. *See also* massive layoff.

workers' comp EAP A new form of **employee assistance program** designed to help employers and injured employees address the emotional and psychological aspects of workplace injuries to speed up claims procedures, keep employees satisfied, and avoid lawsuits. It involves one-on-one counseling by trained counselors who act as liaisons between workers who file workers' compensation claims and claims adjustors; determine what, if any, emotional needs exist; and provide treatment and follow-up.

workers' compensation Statutes passed by all states designed to protect workers from the hazards and consequences of accidents, injuries, illnesses, and death to themselves and their families as a result of their employment. Benefits are paid to workers suffering job-related physical, mental, or emotional accidents, injuries, disabilities, or disfigurement or who aggravate preexisting physical or mental conditions at work. In addition to death benefits, they typically include weekly payments, based on earnings and size of family, for medical and hospital bills, scheduled loss (amputation, loss of use, or loss of a bodily function), payments for scarring, rehabilitation, retraining, settlements, travel expenses, and attorney fees paid to the employee or his or her surviving spouse or children. Businesses must either have adequate funds to pay claims or carry appropriate workers' compensation insurance coverage. The laws also provide some protection to employers against excessive liability.

work hardening Four- to six-week programs provided for injured workers following physical or occupational therapy to give them the self-confidence and stamina needed to resume an active role in the work force. Frequently simulates the work that got employees injured in

the first place to get them back on the job. *See also* industrial rehabilitation.

Work Hours Act of 1962 (WHA) Mandates that wages be computed on
the basis of an 8–hour day, 40–hour week, with payment of overtime for all hours in excess of the basic day and week to certain
classes of laborers.

work injury reports (WIRs) Used by the Bureau of Statistics, U.S. Department of Labor, to identify and describe in WIR surveys the occupational injury and illness situation in the United States. Reports
show the number of injured workers in various categories and the
percentage who reported that they did not receive safety training
for the tasks they were performing when injured.

work measurement A method of determining the amount of output
produced by a specific amount of input during a set period of time.
It involves these steps: definition of the basic units of measurement
(for example, words per minute); development of data collection instruments and procedures; collection, tabulation, and analysis of
work data; definition of work standards; and implementation, follow-up, and (when necessary) revision of the new standards. *See
also* work distribution chart; work simplification.

work methods analysis The process of analyzing procedures, operations, and systems, establishing standards of performance, and
controlling performance to reduce labor costs. It involves systematic
study of each job in an organizational element or process to eliminate unnecessary operations, standardize equipment tools, procedures, and working conditions, and measure the time required to
perform each operation. *See also* work measurement.

workplace know-how Five competencies identified by the Secretary of
Labor's **Commission on Achieving Necessary Skills**. In 1991 it reported that children must master the following: (1) resources—allocating time, money, materials, space, and staff; (2) interpersonal
skills—working on teams, teaching others, serving customers, leading, negotiating, and working well with people from culturally diverse backgrounds; (3) information—how to acquire and process
data, including file management and computer literacy; (4) systems—understanding social, organizational and technological systems, monitoring and correcting performance and designing or improving systems; and (5) technology—selecting equipment and
tools, applying technology to specific tasks and maintaining and
troubleshooting technologies. In addition, the commission stated
that young people also need a foundation that stresses thinking
skills: being able to make decisions, solve problems, and reason.

work process chart A work simplification technique that documents the flow of a single unit (form, document, equipment part, component of a system) through an operation, series of operations, or series of workstations, and enables analysis of the process and subsequent improvement of efficiency. Symbols are used to create a chart showing stages in the work process: operation, transportation, inspection, and storage or delay.

work sharing An alternative to layoffs during recessions or restructuring in which all or part of a company's work force temporarily reduces hours and salary. In some states, employees can collect unemployment insurance to offset part of the wages lost. *See also* compressed workweek; flexiplace; flextime; home worker; job sharing/job splitting; phased retirement; V-time programs.

work simplification A systematic attempt to improve the way work is performed. Its goal is to make work simpler and easier to do. It uses work distribution, work flow, and work process charts to determine exactly how a duty or task is performed; reviews, analyzes, questions, and challenges every step in the work process; develops and tests alternative methods; implements the best and most workable methods; modifies the new method as needed; and repeats the process after an appropriate period of time. *See also* work measurement.

work stoppage Cessation of work by employees in sympathy with a cause or to express a grievance.

work-to-the-rule A tactic used by members of collective bargaining units to underscore their dissatisfaction with management policies or practices. Instead of going on strike, the workers refuse to engage in any work-related activities that are not specifically identified in the labor contract as their responsibility. For example, unionized teachers have expressed their frustration and anger over low salaries, layoffs, imposed pay cuts, and larger class sizes by refusing to write letters of recommendation for student applicants for college admission and scholarships, and to engage in after-school tutoring, evening parent interviews, and club sponsorship.

wrongful discharge Unfair or unjust termination. A corollary to the legal doctrine of "employment-at-will." In a decision by the Supreme Court in June 1988, employees covered by a collective bargaining agreement who have bargained for grievance and arbitration of discharges that violate their contracts have the additional remedy of going to court to sue for compensatory and punitive damages. There are three basic grounds for such a suit: breach of contract, violation of public policy, and breach of an implied covenant of good faith and fair dealing. *See also* employment-at-will; retaliatory discharge.

X

Xers A label for a generation, a demographic generalization applied to the generation following the **baby boomers**, the group brought up on video and accustomed to technology, that came of age in the late 1980s and early 1990s. Said to be pragmatic, highly competitive, self- and fulfillment-oriented. Attributed to Douglas Copeland in the novel *Generation X: Tales for an Accelerated Society. See also* baby busters.

Y

yellow-dog contract An agreement not to join a union forced on employees before they were hired by employers. The practice was prevalent in the early days of unions (prior to the 1930s), but it is now illegal. *See also* Labor-Management Relations Act of 1947.

yiffies Translates to "young, individualistic, freedom-minded and few" persons. Applies to persons under 26 who decide for themselves where they're going, are not totally dedicated to their jobs, and are in the post-1964 generation of people more interested in job satisfaction, a laid-back life-style, and having fun than they are in money.

Z

Z-list Four tables of hazardous substances identified in the OSHA Hazard Communication Standard. The list is available from the Superintendent of Documents, U.S. Government Printing Office, Washington, DC 20402-9325.